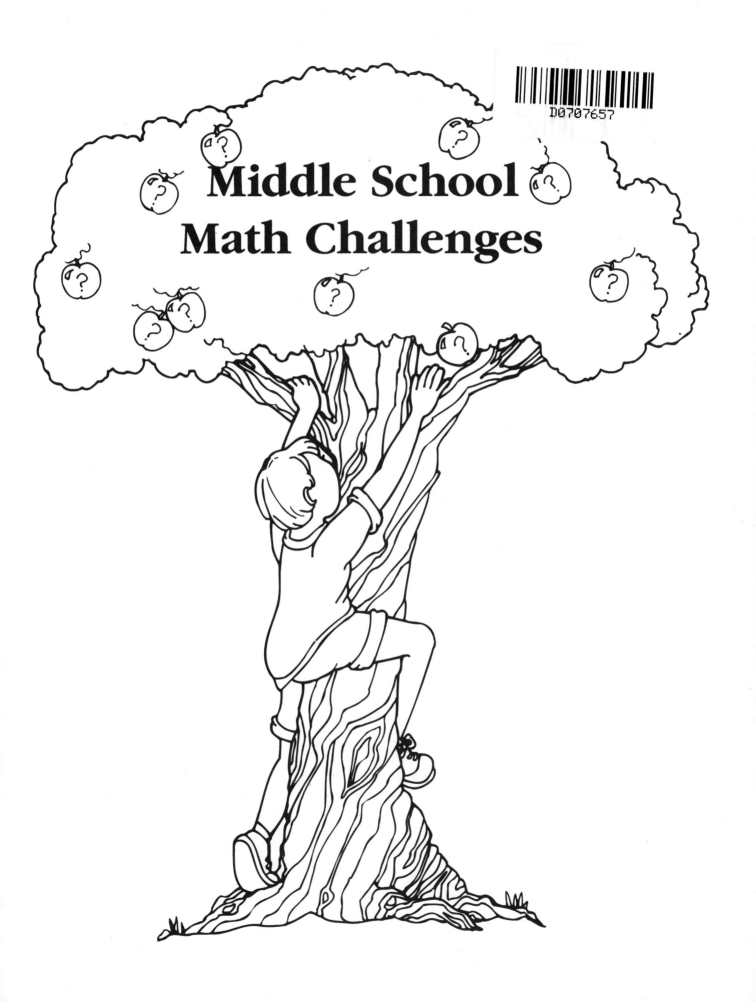

Middle School
Math Challenges

Middle School Math Challenges
Grades 5–8

Editor: Donna Borst
Illustrator: Janet Armbrust
Cover Design: Tom Sjoerdsma

GOOD APPLE
A Division of Frank Schaffer Publications, Inc.
23740 Hawthorne Blvd.
Torrance, CA 90505

ISBN 1-56417-967-2

Table of Contents

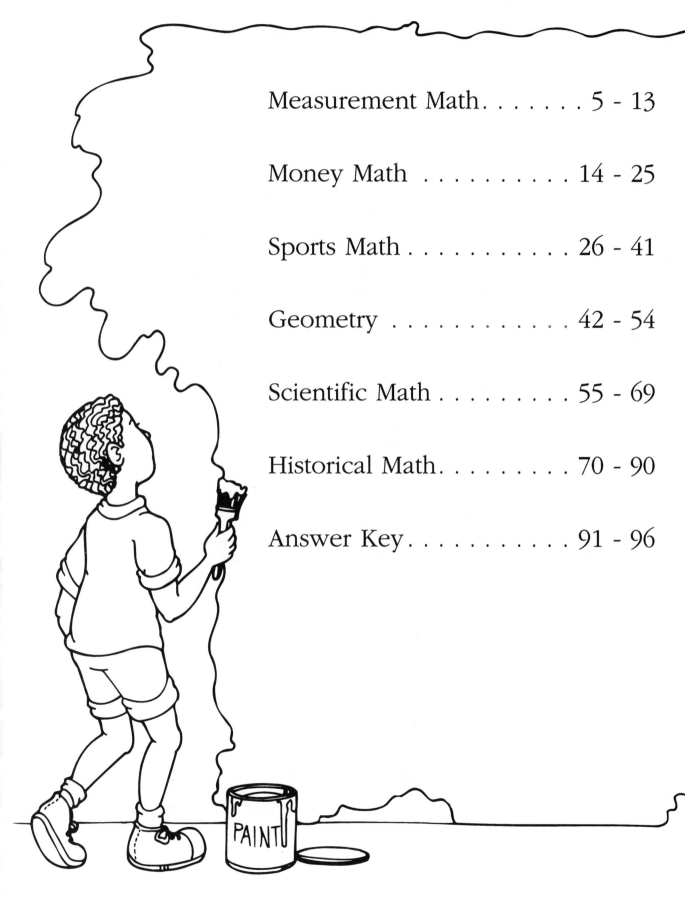

To the Teacher,

The title of this book really says it all. The reproducible worksheets in this resource will challenge your middle school students and entertain them as well. Every student will find something interesting in this unique resource. Measurement math, money math, sports math, scientific math, historical math, and geometry make up this terrific resource compiled from past issues of *Oasis* magazine. While reinforcing math skills, students will learn more about the environment, the solar system, dinosaurs, the Civil War, insects, and the Wright Brothers. They will read stock tables, use a variety of graphs, find the perimeter of a baseball diamond, and help out with budgets. Middle school math has never been more fun, and the combination of math and other subject areas, makes this book a one-of-a-kind resource.

After all of these years, *Oasis* continues to be one of the most creative and thought-provoking teacher resources available for middle school students. Each issue is filled with activities, reproducibles, and units for every subject area. Perhaps the best thing of all is that every idea, activity, and unit has been written by teachers just like you. These are people who know what works in the classroom and what doesn't — people who realize that teachers don't have all day to prepare for one lesson and who know the value of making learning fun. If you have ideas that you would like to share with other middle school teachers through *Oasis*, we would love to hear from you. You may submit your ideas to *Oasis*, 3427 Pheasant Run Drive, Wever, IA 52658. If you would like to subscribe to *Oasis*, please call 1-800-264-9873.

GA1610 Good Apple © 1997

Take an Inch

There is an old saying, "Give them an inch and they will take a mile." In this exercise, take some common distances and convert them to inches.

_____ 1. Jack wins a 100-yard dash. How many inches does he cover?

_____ 2. Jill wins a 100-meter (1 meter = 39.37 inches) race. How many inches does she cover?

_____ 3. Bill runs half the length of the football field (50 yards) and scores a touchdown. How many inches does Bill run?

_____ 4. Cheri dribbles the ball the entire length of the basketball court (94 feet) and scores a basket. How many inches does she dribble?

_____ 5. Jason throws a pass across the basketball court (50 feet). How many inches does the pass travel?

_____ 6. Tom hits a home run that travels 390 feet and wins the game. How many inches does the ball travel?

_____ 7. Al Unser, Jr., wins the Indianapolis 500 (500 miles). How many inches does he travel if a mile is 5,280 feet?

continued

Take an Inch

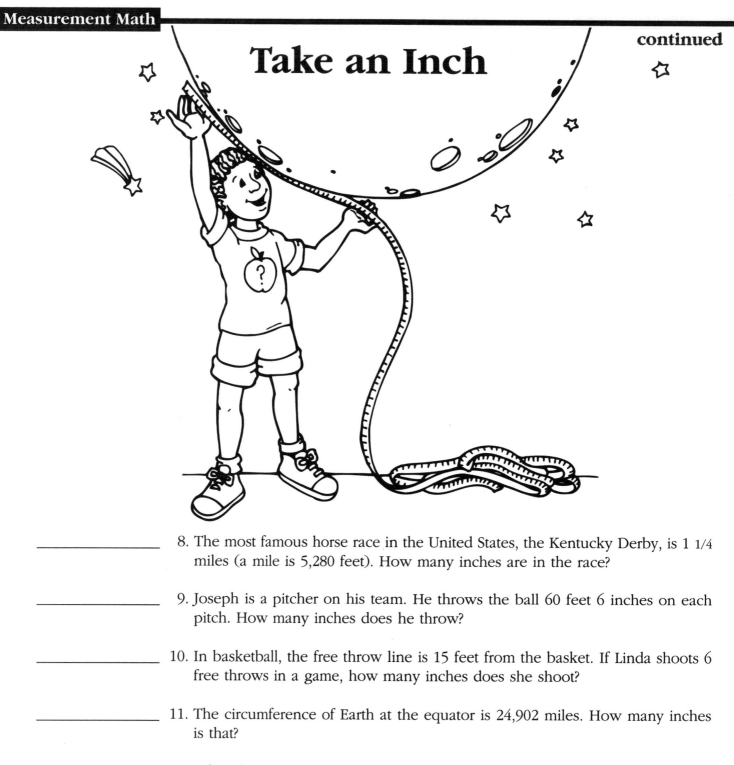

_____ 8. The most famous horse race in the United States, the Kentucky Derby, is 1 1/4 miles (a mile is 5,280 feet). How many inches are in the race?

_____ 9. Joseph is a pitcher on his team. He throws the ball 60 feet 6 inches on each pitch. How many inches does he throw?

_____ 10. In basketball, the free throw line is 15 feet from the basket. If Linda shoots 6 free throws in a game, how many inches does she shoot?

_____ 11. The circumference of Earth at the equator is 24,902 miles. How many inches is that?

_____ 12. Adam lives 100 miles from his grandparents' home. How many inches must he travel to visit them?

_____ 13. The diameter of the moon is 2,160 miles. How many inches is that?

_____ 14. How many fewer inches is the moon's diameter than Earth's? (See questions 11 and 13.)

_____ 15. At one time the national debt of the United States was about $4 trillion. Did any of your answers equal 4 trillion inches?

GA1610 Good Apple © 1997

How Do You Measure Up?

In each of the statements below, only one answer is correct. Test your measurement accuracy by circling the correct ending to each statement.

1. In his early years, George Washington was a surveyor. Mr. Washington measured _____.
   a. time   b. space   c. weight

2. The measurement of force and motion in automobiles is in _____.
   a. knots   b. friction   c. horsepower

3. The metric system fits into _____.
   a. fractions   b. Roman numerals   c. decimals

4. A light year (the distance traveled by a ray of light in one year) is about _____.
   a. 240,000 miles   b. 6,000,000,000,000 miles   c. 93,000,000 miles

5. Land is measured in _____.
   a. pecks   b. acres   c. furlongs

6. A yard is _____.
   a. slightly more than a meter b. the same as a meter   c. slightly less than a meter

7. Canada measures liquid in imperial gallons. An imperial gallon is about _____.
   a. one-fifth larger than   b. one-fifth less than   c. the same as
      a United States gallon   a United States gallon   a United States gallon

8. A short ton is 2,000 pounds. A long ton is _____.
   a. 2,204.5 pounds   b. 2,100 pounds   c. 2,240 pounds

9. Two systems of measuring temperatures are _____.
   a. centigrade and pyrometers b. Celsius and Fahrenheit   c. centigrade and absolute zero

10. A photographer would use a _____.
   a. light meter   b. voltmeter   c. barometer

continued

How Do You Measure Up?

11. An airplane pilot would use a(n) _____.
    a. altimeter   b. meter   c. thermometer

12. The measurement a scuba diver would be interested in would be a _____.
    a. pound   b. carat   c. fathom

13. A hiker would use a _____.
    a. manometer   b. tachometer   c. pedometer

14. The depth of water can be measured by a _____.
    a. chronometer   b. Fathometer   c. water clock

15. A man with a forest sells wood by the _____.
    a. cord   b. hundredweight   c. gross

16. Leap year comes every four years. It makes February _____.
    a. one day shorter   b. four days longer   c. one day longer

17. A druggist uses _____.
    a. apothecaries' weight   b. troy weight   c. avoirdupois weight

18. A diamond is measured by _____.
    a. calories   b. carats   c. cubits

19. Absolute zero and the boiling point are measurements of _____.
    a. electricity   b. temperature   c. distance

20. One item which does not measure is a _____.
    a. sextant   b. hydrometer   c. measuring worm

8

Measurement Match

Match each measurement with its correct definition by placing the letter of that definition on the blank next to the name of the measurement.

_____	1. cubit	a. 2,000 pounds
_____	2. fathom	b. the millionth part of a meter
_____	3. hogshead	c. highest point
_____	4. league	d. about 18 inches
_____	5. micron	e. 2,240 pounds
_____	6. vertex	f. 63 gallons
_____	7. gram	g. measure of weight for precious stones
_____	8. carat	h. nautical measure—6 feet
_____	9. short ton	i. metric unit equal to 15.432 grains
_____	10. long ton	j. 3 miles
_____	11. barometer	k. device which shows time by shadow
_____	12. chronometer	l. measures speed
_____	13. galvanometer	m. records weight or pressure of atmosphere
_____	14. hydrometer	n. accurate timekeeper
_____	15. pendulum	o. measures altitude of heavenly bodies
_____	16. sextant	p. measures strengths of liquids
_____	17. spirometer	q. rod which regulates movements of a clock
_____	18. sundial	r. measures strength and direction of electric current
_____	19. tachometer	s. measures angular distances
_____	20. quadrant	t. measures amount of oxygen a person's body uses

Measurement Math

Write the correct answer in the blank at the left of each statement.

_____ 1. A section of land is 640 acres. How much is a quarter section?

_____ 2. There are 160 square rods in an acre. How many square rods are there in a section of land?

_____ 3. Light travels 186,000 miles per second. How many miles would it travel in one hour?

_____ 4. The sun is about 93,000,000 miles from Earth. Approximately how long does it take for light from the sun to reach Earth?

_____ 5. The moon is approximately 240,000 miles from Earth. How long does it take for light from the moon to reach Earth?

_____ 6. A gallon of paint will cover 400 square feet. A man needs enough paint to cover 4,000 square feet. If a gallon of paint costs $8.95, what will be the total cost of the paint?

_____ 7. A hectare is 2.471 acres. If a woman sells 10 hectares at $100 an acre, how much money will she receive?

_____ 8. A mile is 5,280 feet. How many inches are in a mile? How many yards?

_____ 9. A furlong is 220 yards. A horse runs 7 furlongs. How many feet does it run?

_____ 10. Add a kilometer (0.62137 of a mile) and a knot (1.15 of a mile). How many miles are in the total?

GA1610 Good Apple © 1997

Measurement Math

Write the correct answer in the blank at the left of each statement.

_____ 11. A farmer sold his farm for $160,000. He got $60,000 for the house and $1,000 per acre for his land. How many acres did he sell?

_____ 12. The distance between two ports is 3,300 miles. *Ship A* sails at 20 knots per hour, *Ship B* at 26 knots. How much sooner (to the nearest hour) will *Ship B* arrive than *Ship A*?

_____ 13. A fathom is 6 feet. A league is equal to 3 miles. Which is longer—25,000 fathoms or 30 leagues?

_____ 14. The circumference of the world is approximately 25,000 miles. If a ship covers 10 leagues an hour, how many days will it take to circle the globe?

_____ 15. There are 4 pecks in a bushel. A man sells tomatoes at $1.00 per bushel or 30 cents a peck. How much money will a customer save if he buys 100 bushels instead of 400 pecks?

_____ 16. A man buys a hogshead (63 gallons) of mineral water for $4.00 a gallon and sells it for $1.50 a quart. What is his profit?

_____ 17. A house with 3,600 square feet is sold for $150,000. What is the price per square foot?

_____ 18. Richard Petty wins a 500-mile race in 4 hours. How many feet per minute was his car traveling?

_____ 19. John, Mary, and Bill run a race. John runs 880 yards, Mary 805 meters, and Bill 2,640 feet. Who runs the greatest distance?

_____ 20. Just for fun: If a snail can cover a mile in 10 hours and a rabbit can cover a mile in 2 minutes, how much of a head start could a rabbit give a snail in a mile race and still win? Specify your answer in hours, minutes, and seconds.

A FATHOM IS SIX FEET

Metric Mathematics

Write the correct answer in the blank at the left of each statement.
(Answers may vary slightly depending on the conversion factor used.)

_____ 1. Yarditia went to the grocery store and ordered a pound of bacon. The reply was, "We don't sell bacon by the pound, we sell it by the gram." If a pound of bacon is 16 ounces, how many grams would this be?

_____ 2. "More snow and more snow," said Milli Meter. "Monday, we had 32 inches; Tuesday, 25 centimeters; Wednesday, one foot; Thursday, 1 meter; and Friday, 10 inches." How much snow had fallen from Monday through Friday in meters, and what was the average daily snowfall in inches?

_____ 3. Ms. Meter said to the class, "If Johnny Foot walked 54 feet to meet Jennie Gram, how many centimeters did he walk?"

_____ 4. If you threw a Frisbee 50'6", how many millimeters would it go?

_____ 5. Jennie and Jimmy Gram entered a walkathon. Both of them did the following amounts of walking: Jennie Gram walked 10 kilometers and 15 miles, Jimmy Gram walked 5,280 feet and 5 kilometers. What was the total amount of the walks in kilometers?

_____ 6. Jennie Kilo swam 390 inches one day, and the next day she swam 15.8 meters. Her brother swam 1010.1 inches in two days. What's the difference between the two swimmers' distances, in inches?

_____ 7. A train was going 100 miles per hour, and it slowed down to 40 miles per hour. How much did it slow down, in kilometers per hour?

_____ 8. On Monday, it was 40° Celsius; Tuesday, 108° Fahrenheit; Wednesday, 45° Celsius; and only 100° Fahrenheit today. Convert the above temperatures to the nearest full degree of either Celsius or Fahrenheit.

_____ 9. A liter of gas costs about 70 cents in Montreal. How many liters are in a gallon? If you get 45 liters of gas, what is the price of the gasoline?

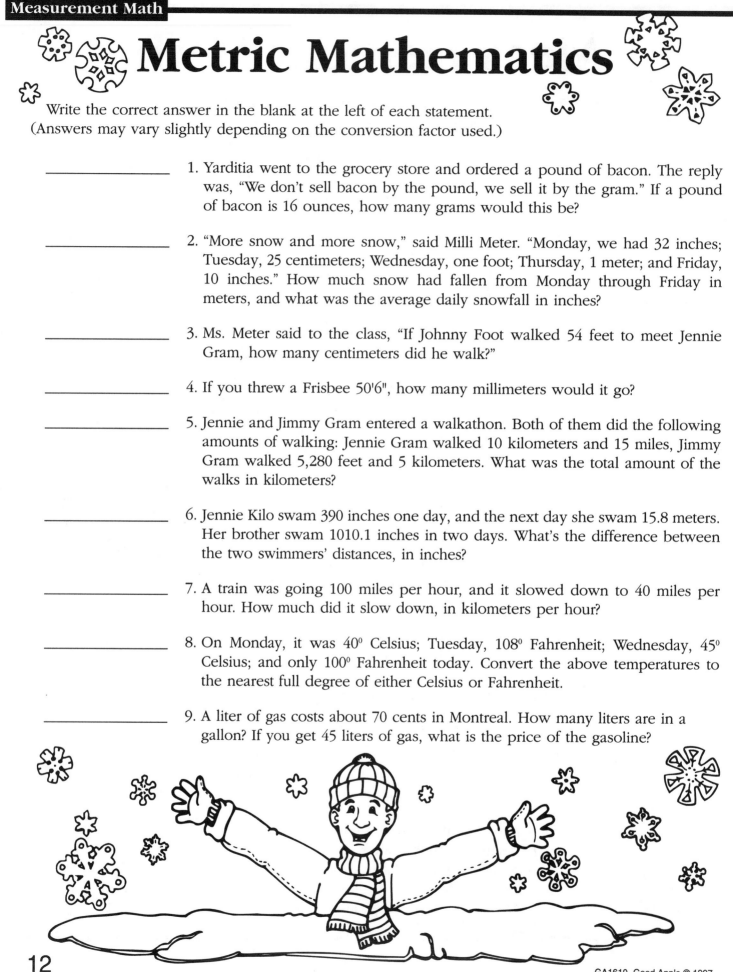

12

Matching Measurements

Match those items which are equal.

_____ 1. 72 inches	a. 90 minutes
_____ 2. 1 1/2 cups	b. 9 square feet
_____ 3. 5,280 feet	c. 36 hours
_____ 4. 10 years	d. 120 inches
_____ 5. 1 1/2 pounds	e. 1 tablespoon
_____ 6. 1 quart	f. 8 ounces
_____ 7. 10 feet	g. 2 yards
_____ 8. 2 hours	h. 200 years
_____ 9. 2 days	i. 120 minutes
_____ 10. 2 centuries	j. 1 pound
_____ 11. 1 square yard	k. 48 hours
_____ 12. 3 teaspoons	l. 24 ounces
_____ 13. 16 ounces	m. half a gallon
_____ 14. 1 cup	n. a decade
_____ 15. 4 quarts	o. a mile
_____ 16. 1 1/2 days	p. 2 pints
_____ 17. 1/4 cup	q. 1 gallon
_____ 18. 4 pecks	r. 12 ounces
_____ 19. 1 1/2 hours	s. a bushel
_____ 20. 2 quarts	t. 4 tablespoons

Numismatic Numbers

Numismatics (coin collecting) is a hobby that everyone, from young to old, can enjoy. Collecting pennies, nickels, or dimes is affordable to youngsters while some adults may pay more than $100,000 for one coin. Become a numismatist by solving these problems.

_____ 1. A coin's value is determined by age, rarity (how many were made), and condition.
_____   An 1851 large cent costs $23.50. In uncirculated condition, it costs $195.
                   a) What is the cost difference? b) What is the percentage difference?

_____ 2. An 1849 gold dollar listed as *fine* costs $140. In the highest grade it costs $12,000.
                   About how many more times does the highest grade cost than the fine condition?

_____ 3. A $20 double eagle gold coin costs $90,000 in its highest grade. What is the
                   difference between the face value and the cost now?

_____ 4. Coins are minted (made) in different places in the United States. A 1913 D
                   (Denver) nickel costs $85. A 1913 S (San Francisco) nickel costs $90. How much
                   would it cost to buy 10 of each coin?

_____ 5. Over the years, mints have made gold coins in the following denominations: $1,
                   $2 1/2, $3, $5, $10, $20. What is the total of these coins?

_____ 6. In the top grade, these coins now sell for the following prices: $1: $14,000;
                   $2 1/2: $8,200; $3: $23,000; $5: $12,000; $10: $15,000; $20: $11,000. What is the
                   total of the top grade gold coins?

_____ 7. The mints make mint sets for collectors consisting of 50¢, 25¢, 10¢, 5¢, and 1¢
                   coins. If a 1975 mint set sells for $4.50, what is the difference between the face
                   value and selling cost?

_____ 8. A dealer buys a coin for $206 and sells it for $214. What is the percentage of
                   profit? Round your answer.

_____ 9. A dealer buys a roll of 50 coins for $550. What is the cost of each coin?

_____ 10. The mint makes special polished coins called proof sets. A proof set for 1950 costs
                    $450. For 1988, $19.75. Is the 1950 set worth 45 times more than the 1988 set?

GA1610 Good Apple © 1997

Numismatic Numbers

_____ 11. A dealer will sell one coin for $24 or 10 coins for $230. How much will the buyer save per coin by buying 10?

_____ 12. Mints make commemorative coins (to recognize special events such as the 200th anniversary of the Constitution). A $1 proof Constitution set costs $14. How much would 130 sets cost?

_____ 13. A bag of 5,000 cents costs $275. What is the approximate cost per cent?

_____ 14. A coin newspaper costs $4 for 13 weeks. What is the approximate cost per week?

_____ 15. A dealer sells 10-ounce silver bars at 39¢ per ounce profit. If he sells 200 ounces, how much profit does he make?

_____ 16. A coin dealer takes a full-page ad in a coin newspaper. The cost is $1,701. However, she gets a 20% discount. What does she pay for the ad?

_____ 17. A coin collector orders 40 coins at 18¢ each. He pays 4% sales tax and $1.50 postage. What is the total amount for the order?

_____ 18. A girl buys 65 different mercury dimes for $62. She gets a 5% discount. What was her final cost per coin?

_____ 19. A dealer advertises that she is going out of business. She is selling 400,000 coins for $1,000,000. How much is that per coin?

_____ 20. An 1804 silver dollar (only 15 exist) is expected to sell for $1,000,000. What is the approximate percent of increase in value per year (in 1997) since it was minted (made)?

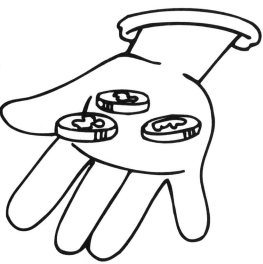

Family Budgets

All families need a budget to keep up with their expenses and to use their income wisely. Help the Smith family with its budget planning.

_____ 1. Mr. Smith's salary is $35,873. His wife's salary is $32,870. What is their combined income?

_____ 2. In addition to their salaries, the Smiths receive $990 in stock dividends and $1,400 in interest from a savings account each year. What is their total income?

_____ 3. Mr. Smith's weekly salary is $689. He has the following deductions withheld from his check: 15% federal income tax, 7.2% social security, and 5% state tax. What is his take-home pay?

_____ 4. Mrs. Smith's annual salary is $32,870. What is her gross weekly pay (to the nearest dollar)?

_____ 5. If Mrs. Smith's percentage of federal income tax, state tax, and social security are the same as her husband's, what is her take-home pay?

_____ 6. What is the combined take-home pay of Mr. and Mrs. Smith per week?

_____ 7. The Smiths spend $400 per month for food. What percent of their combined take-home pay goes for food?

_____ 8. Their house payments are $800 per month. What percent of their combined take-home pay goes for house payments?

_____ 9. Car expenses are $250 per month. What percentage of their take-home pay goes for car expenses?

_____ 10. The Smiths spend $4,800 per year on child care. How much is that per month?

Family Budgets

11. The Smiths spend 5% of their take-home pay on utilities.
    a) How much is that per month?

    _____

    b) Per year (figure using 12 months)?

    _____

12. The Smiths spend $80, $77, $65, and $56, which they label as miscellaneous expenses. What is the total?

    _____

13. The Smiths spend $590 per month on entertainment and vacations. What does that average per day for March?

    _____

14. The Smiths save 6% from each of their paychecks.
    a) What does that average per week?

    _____

    b) Per year?

    _____

15. The Smiths can deduct $8,000 for dependents from their federal income tax obligations. They get $5,000 more for personal deductions. Subtract this total from the Smiths' yearly gross income. What is the figure on which they will pay income tax?

    _____

16. They must pay 15% tax on the first $34,000 they earn and 28% on all income over that amount. How much tax will they pay?

    _____

17. The Smiths have assets of $197,000 and liabilities of $94,850. What is their net worth?

    _____

18. Their house is 50% of their assets. How much is the house worth?

    _____

19. The Smiths still owe $88,560 mortgage on their house. How much of the house actually belongs to them?

    _____

20. The Smiths have $25,000 in savings, $9,600 in stocks, and $6,600 in an IRA.
    a) What are their total savings?

    _____

    b) About how many months' take-home pay do the Smiths have in savings?

Reading Stock Tables

In the business section of the newspaper, you will find the stock listings. They look like this:

52 week					Sales				
High	**Low**	**Stock**	**Div**	**PE**	**100s**	**High**	**Low**	**Last**	**Chg.**
36 5/8	20 5/8	AAR	.50	24	890	36 5/8	34 5/8	35 5/8	+5/8
[1]		[2]	[3]	[4]	[5]	[6]		[7]	

[1.] Price range showing highest and lowest prices per share paid on the Exchange during the year.

[2.] Abbreviation for name of corporation issuing the stock.

[3.] Rate of annual dividend.

[4.] Price of a share of stock divided by earnings per share for a 12-month period.

[5.] Number of shares traded expressed in 100s – e.g. for this stock 89,000. Odd lot quantities are not included unless a letter "z" precedes the entry.

[6.] The highest price paid for this security during the day was $36.62 1/2 and the lowest was $34.62 1/2 .

[7.] The closing price (or last sale of the day) of this stock was $35.62 1/2 . This was $.62 1/2 more than the closing price of the day before.

Reading Stock Tables

52 week High	Low	Stock	Div	PE	Sales 100s	High	Low	Last	Chg.
67 1/8	40 3/8	DeltaAr	1.20	10	10870	59 5/8	56 3/4	56 1/2	-1 3/4
30 1/4	17 7/8	Dexter	.60	19	z1863	29 7/8	28 5/8	29 7/8	+1/2
81 5/8	36	Disney	.32	29	20003	81 5/8	77	81 5/8	+2 3/4
100 7/8	51 7/8	DowCh	2.20	21	37241	100 7/8	95	99 3/4	+1 7/8
40	28	EGG	.56	23	2327	39 7/8	38	.39 1/2	-1/8

1. In the last year, what was the highest price paid for Disney stock? _____

2. a. How much dividend is paid by DeltaAr stocks? _____

   b. How much dividend is paid by EGG stocks? _____

3. Exactly how many shares were traded for the following stocks: a. Dexter _____

   b. DowCH _____

   c. EGG _____

4. If someone bought 100 shares of the following stocks at the following prices, how much money would he or she have made or lost by selling that stock during the last sale of the day today?

   a. DeltaAR at $59.00 _____

   b. Dexter at $29.50 _____

   c. Disney at $79.00 _____

   d. DowCh at $100.00 _____

5. a. Which of the above stocks went up the most in price? _____

   b. Which of the above stocks went down the most? _____

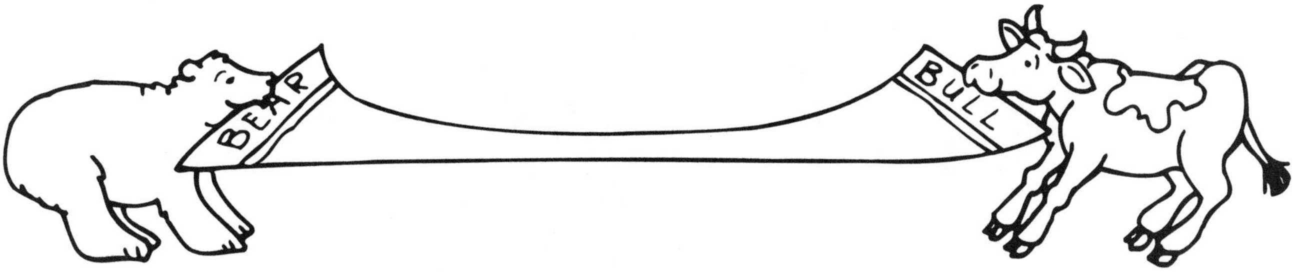

Money Math

Read the following sentences and answer the questions. Refer to an encyclopedia or almanac for help.

1. Each $1 bills stays in circulation for 1 1/2 years.

_____ a. How many months is a $1 bill in circulation?

_____ b. Whose picture is on a $1 bill?

_____ c. What picture is on the reverse side of a $1 bill?

2. Each $5 bill stays in circulation 6 months longer than a $1 bill.

_____ a. How long does a $5 bill stay in circulation?

_____ b. Whose picture is on a $5 bill?

_____ c. What picture is on the reverse side of a $5 bill?

3. Each $2 bill stays in circulation 18 times longer than a $5 bill.

_____ a. How long does a $2 bill stay in circulation?

_____ b. Whose picture is on a $2 bill?

_____ c. What picture is on the reverse side of a $2 bill?

4. Each $10 bill stays in circulation twice as long as a $1 bill.

_____ a. How long does a $10 bill stay in circulation?

_____ b. Whose picture is on a $10 bill?

_____ c. What picture is on the reverse side of a $10 bill?

5. Each $20 bill stays in circulation 5 years.

_____ a. How many months is a $20 bill in circulation?

_____ b. Whose picture is on a $20 bill?

_____ c. What picture is on the reverse side of a $20 bill?

Money Math

6. Each $50 bill stays in circulation three times longer than a $10 bill.

_____   a. How long does a $50 bill stay in circulation?

_____   b. Whose picture is on a $50 bill?

_____   c. What picture is on the reverse side of a $50 bill?

7. Each $100 bill stays in circulation four times longer than a $20 bill.

_____   a. How long does a $100 bill stay in circulation?

_____   b. Whose picture is on a $100 bill?

_____   c. What picture is on the reverse side of a $100 bill?

8. United States dollars are printed on 75% cotton and the rest is linen.

_____   a. Linen makes up a what percent of a bill?

_____   b. What government agency prints currency?

_____   c. Where is it located?

9. All United States bills carry the same motto.

_____   a. What is the motto on each bill?

_____   b. What color are all bills?

_____   c. What is the size of all bills?

10. If 2/5 of a bill is damaged, it can be redeemed for its full value.

_____   a. How much of a bill is needed to receive its full value?

_____   b. Who is responsible for the prevention of counterfeiting?

_____   c. What two signatures appear on all bills?

Making Change

You are a clerk in a department store, and the following purchases pass through your register. What denominations (coins or bills) of money and in what order would you give the change to each customer?

_____ 1. Kathy's bill comes to $5.95 plus she owes 30¢ tax. She gives you two $5 bills. Her change is?

_____ 2. The bill for Tyler's tennis racket comes to $23. There is also $1.15 owed in tax. Tyler gives you a $20 bill and a $10 bill. What's his change?

_____ 3. George spends $37.87 (including tax). He gives you a $50 bill. What do you give him?

_____ 4. Angie buys a shirt for $14. Tax on it comes to 70¢. She gives you a $20 bill. What change does Angie receive?

_____ 5. A number of small items Barb purchases total $16.20. If sales tax amounts to 81¢ and Barb gives you a $20 bill, figure her change.

_____ 6. Janie brings to your register a sweater marked $21 that is on sale at a 25% discount and a blouse that says $18 but is 1/3 off. Janie hands you two $10 and two $5 dollar bills. What kind of change does she get? (Don't forget the 6% sales tax.)

_____ 7. Kim buys a radio that is marked $39.95. But there is a sign beside the radio that reads "Sale—$5.00 off regular price." If the tax is $2.08, what kind of change does Kim get from two $20 bills?

_____ 8. Marty purchases a stuffed rabbit for his little brother that was marked $9.95. You know that sales tax is 6%. He offers you two $5 bills plus a single. What change does Marty get?

_____ 9. Tom buys two compact discs that sell for $7.95 each. There is also 6% sales tax to be computed. If Tom gives you two $10 dollar bills, what kind of change should he get?

_____ 10. Your final customer, Diamond Jim, is the "big spender" of the day. Jim purchases a total of $86.79 in merchandise. He pays for it with a $100 bill. Calculate Diamond Jim's change.

GA1610 Good Apple © 1997

Shopping Savvy

Sam is having a super storewide sale. Compute your savings and fill in the missing values.

Items	Price	Sale	Savings	Change from $25.00
Cassette Tape	$10.98	$9.99		
Shampoo	3.59	2.98		
Sweatshirt	14.50	10.98		
Notebook	2.49	1.79		
Sunglasses	8.50	6.89		
Decals	1.15	.99		
Posters	4.49	3.98		
Mugs	3.98	3.47		
Backpacks	22.39	19.99		

Art's Appliances

Do the work on the back of this page. Write your answers in the blanks.

_____ 1. Mr. Jessup brought a refrigerator-freezer and a TV. He paid $150 down. How much did he have left to pay?

_____ 2. After buying over $500 in merchandise from the appliance store, Mr. Carlson got a $25 discount on a vacuum. How much did the vacuum cost?

_____ 3. Sally saved $50. She bought her mom a coffee maker. How much money did she have left?

_____ 4. What is the total cost of the seven items priced in this ad?

_____ 5. The Hydes saved $1,000. They spent $500 on furniture. They also want a new refrigerator-freezer and a TV. How much more money will they have to save before they can buy them?

_____ 6. The store accidentally got a double shipment of refrigerator-freezers. To get rid of them, they sold them for $75 off. What was the sale price?

GA1610 Good Apple © 1997

Tours by Train

People can plan tours by train. Canada is a favorite destination. Compare the following two trips. Then answer the questions based on the information provided.

A. A 10-day tour of Nova Scotia costs $995 per person based on double occupancy (sleeping quarters for two). The trip begins in Toronto.

B. A 4-day trip to Quebec (city) costs $395 per person, also based on double occupancy. This trip also begins in Toronto.

_____ 1. What is the cost per day of the Nova Scotia trip?

_____ 2. What is the cost per day of the Quebec trip?

_____ 3. Do you think a person traveling alone would pay more or less than if he or she traveled with a partner?

_____ 4. How much would the Nova Scotia trip be for a couple?

_____ 5. How much would the Nova Scotia trip be for two adults with two children if the children are charged half price?

_____ 6. a. How much would the Quebec trip cost for a couple?

_____ b. For a family with two children if the children are charged half-price?

_____ 7. If a senior citizen received 15% off, what would such a person (based on double occupancy) pay for the Nova Scotia trip?

_____ 8. How much would he or she pay on the Quebec trip?

_____ 9. If Grandma and Grandpa, both senior citizens, accompanied the two-child family on the Nova Scotia trip, what would the total cost be?

_____ 10. What's the total cost for the same family on the Quebec trip?

_____ 11. The Nova Scotia trip is 2,500 miles. What is the average number of miles traveled daily?

_____ 12. The Quebec trip is 332 miles from Toronto to Montreal, then 698 miles from Montreal to Quebec. What is the total mileage?

_____ 13. What is the average number of miles traveled daily in question 12?

_____ 14. Why do you think prices are given as $995 and $395 instead of round numbers $1,000 and $400, a difference of only $5 in each total?

Pictograph

Monday	
Tuesday	
Wednesday	
Thursday	
Friday	
Saturday	

Paid attendance at Belton Junior High Baseball Camp

Each  represents 50 people

1. How many people attended camp on each day it was open? _____

_____

2. Which day had the highest attendance? _____

3. Which day had the lowest attendance? _____

4. On what two days was the total attendance 450? _____

5. What was the difference between the highest and the lowest attendance? _____

6. How many fewer people attended the camp on Saturday than on Friday? _____

7. If the price of admission was 75¢, how much money was collected on Monday and

   Tuesday? _____

8. How much money was collected on the day when attendance was lowest? _____

9. How much was collected on the day when attendance was highest? _____

10. How much money was collected during the entire camp week? _____

Baseball Math

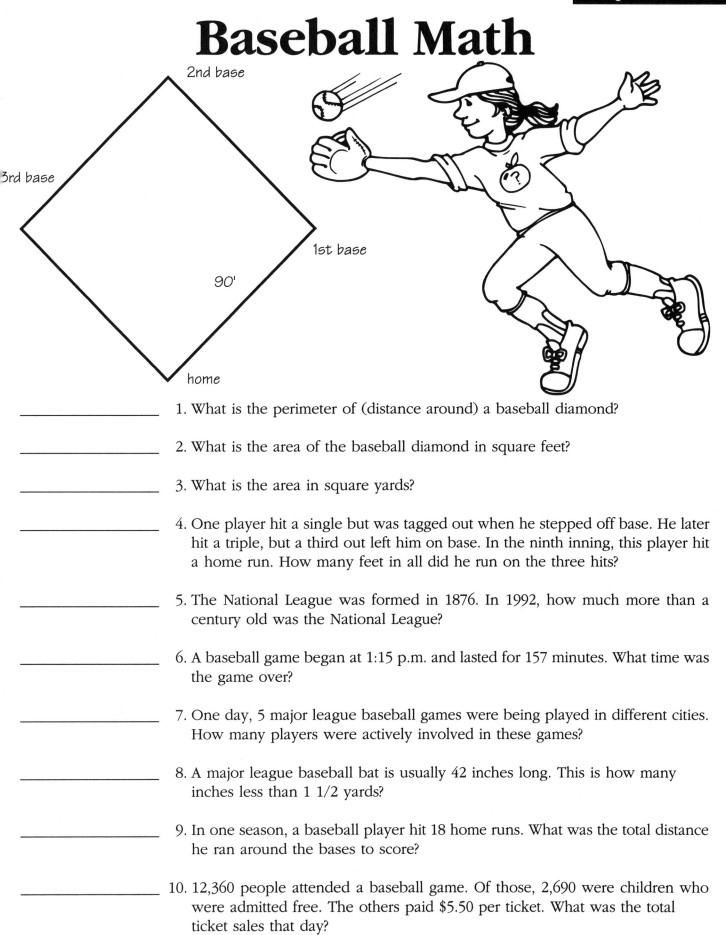

2nd base

3rd base

1st base

90'

home

_____ 1. What is the perimeter of (distance around) a baseball diamond?

_____ 2. What is the area of the baseball diamond in square feet?

_____ 3. What is the area in square yards?

_____ 4. One player hit a single but was tagged out when he stepped off base. He later hit a triple, but a third out left him on base. In the ninth inning, this player hit a home run. How many feet in all did he run on the three hits?

_____ 5. The National League was formed in 1876. In 1992, how much more than a century old was the National League?

_____ 6. A baseball game began at 1:15 p.m. and lasted for 157 minutes. What time was the game over?

_____ 7. One day, 5 major league baseball games were being played in different cities. How many players were actively involved in these games?

_____ 8. A major league baseball bat is usually 42 inches long. This is how many inches less than 1 1/2 yards?

_____ 9. In one season, a baseball player hit 18 home runs. What was the total distance he ran around the bases to score?

_____ 10. 12,360 people attended a baseball game. Of those, 2,690 were children who were admitted free. The others paid $5.50 per ticket. What was the total ticket sales that day?

Bicycle Numbers

Bicycling is a favorite form of recreation for many people of all ages. Some serious bicycle riders travel thousands of miles per year for healthful exercise and sightseeing pleasure. A few elite riders make bicycling a profession. They ride in races all over the world for thousands of dollars in prizes. Rate your bicycle math skills by finding the correct answers to the following problems.

_____ 1. One famous bicycle race is 3,117 miles long. One rider rode 2,450 miles before dropping out of the race. What percent, to the nearest whole number, did he cover before dropping out?

_____ 2. The winning time for the man in that race was 9 days, 11 hours, and 35 minutes. The winning time for the woman who won was 11 days, 21 hours, and 15 minutes. What was the difference between the man's time and the woman's time?

_____ 3. In 1987, 30 states held one or more bicycle races. Approximately what fraction of all the states held races?

_____ 4. Serious bikers must be in excellent physical condition. A 24-year-old man who does not exercise has 15% body fat. A 24-year-old professional cyclist has 8% body fat. If each man weighs 150 pounds, how many pounds of fat does the non-exerciser have? the cyclist?

_____ 5. In a 100-mile race, the first-place winner averages 24 miles per hour. What was the time in hours and minutes? (Round to the nearest minute.)

_____ 6. The last-place finisher in that race averaged 12 miles per hour. What was the time in hours and minutes? (Round to the nearest minute.)

_____ 7. 8,000 bikers entered a race to raise money for charity. 7,999 finished the 20-mile race. One biker dropped out after 8 miles. What was the total number of miles all entrants covered?

_____ 8. 25,000 bikers rode a total of 672,000 miles in a year. What was the average number of miles per person per year? the average number of miles per week?

_____ 9. A bicycle manufacturing company modernized its plant. The first year it spent $23,000,000. It plans to spend 25% more the following year. What will be the total cost of modernization?

_____ 10. A bicycle company produced 600,000 bicycles in 1988 and sold them for an average of $229 per bicycle. (a) What was the total amount of sales? (b) If the company made 15% profit, what was the profit total?

_____ 11. 207 cyclists started an important European race. 135 finished. What percent of those who started finished the race? (To the nearest percent.)

_____ 12. A bicyclist rode 9,000 miles her first year, 6,000 her second year and 7,000 her third year. What was the total mileage for the three years?

_____ 13. The fourth year, the biker rode 11,850 miles; the fifth, 11,857; the sixth, 12,100 miles. How many more miles did she ride in the last three years than the first three years?

Basketball Math

_____ 1. A basketball team won 27 games and lost 3 during the season. What was the team's winning percentage?

_____ 2. A basketball team's free-throw percentage was 65. If the team shot 800 free throws during the season, how many did it make?

_____ 3. A team with a 25-7 record averaged 77 points per game. How many points did the team score for the season?

_____ 4. A team that played 32 games averaged 35 rebounds, and its opponents averaged 36. How many fewer rebounds did the team make than its opponents?

_____ 5. Four teams in the NCAA tournament had the following records: 23-7, 27-3, 24-6, and 23-7. What was the average losing percentage for the four teams? (Round to the nearest percent.)

_____ 6. A team plays 31 games. If the team makes 180 steals, how many steals does it average per game? (Round to the nearest tenth.)

_____ 7. The team with the best record in the NCAA tournament was 27-3. The worst record was 16-13. What was the winning percentage of each?

_____ 8. Team A plays Team B. Team A makes 50% of 68 two-point field goals, 75% of 32 free throws. Team B makes 54% of 75 field goals and 60% of 24 free throws. Which team wins?

_____ 9. If the top scorer in the nation averaged 32.9 points a game for 30 games, how many points did he score?

_____ 10. If the top rebounder averaged 13.6 rebounds per game, how many rebounds did he make in 25 games?

continue

Basketball Math

_____ 11. If the best shooting team in the nation attempted 1,932 field goals and made 57.3%, how many field goals did the team make?

_____ 12. The top woman player for College A scored 2,326 points in 4 years. What was her average per year?

_____ 13. Team A has won many games in the past few years. It has won 63.9% of 227 games. How many games has it won and lost?

_____ 14. Teams that reach the finals in a college tournament will receive $1,250,640. That is 8% more than last year. How much did they receive last year?

_____ 15. Making the 64-team field in a national college tournament is worth at least $250,200. What is the total the 64 teams will receive in the first round?

_____ 16. The women's basketball championship tournament invited 32 teams. Six of these teams were from Southeastern Conferences. What percentage was from the SEC?

_____ 17. The best two-point field-goal shooter on a women's team averages 66.6% of goals attempted. The best three-point shooter averages 42%. If the two-point shooter attempts 24 shots in a game and the three-point shooter attempts 20 shots, which player scores the most points?

_____ 18. Team B averages 106 points a game (48 minutes). How many points does the team score per minute?

_____ 19. Following is the height of Team B's starting team: 6'7", 6'9", 6'10", 6'2", 6'7". What was the total number in inches for the starting five?

_____ 20. There have been 50 college Champions. Team A has won 10, Team B has won 5, and Team C has won 5. How many championships have been won by all other teams?

30

Baseball Math

Any baseball player likes to have a high batting average. The more hits a player gets, the more runs batted in (RBI) and runs (R) he will have to his credit. To find a player's batting average (Avg.), do this:

1. Divide the number of hits (H) a player makes by the number of times at bat (AB).
2. In Example 1, a player batted 185 times and hit safely 58 times. Add a decimal point and four zeros to 58 (58.0000) and divide by 185. The answer is .3135. As batting averages are always given as a three-place number (thousandth), the last digit in the answer, 5, is dropped. Any time a 5 or any number higher (6, 7, 8, 9) is dropped, the third number in the answer (in this example, 3) is increased by 1 (this is sometimes called rounding up or rounding to the nearest thousandth). The batting average is .314.
3. In Example 2, a player made 37 hits in 106 times at bat. Add a decimal and 4 zeros to 37 (37.0000) and divide by 106. The answer is .3490. The 0 is dropped and because it is less than five, the batting average is .349.

Find the batting averages of the players below.

	AB	H	Avg. (4-place answer)	Avg. (rounded to 3 places)
1. Jones	177	54	_____	_____
2. McGill	205	64	_____	_____
3. Adams	178	58	_____	_____
4. Riley	160	46	_____	_____
5. Diaz	138	38	_____	_____

More Baseball Math

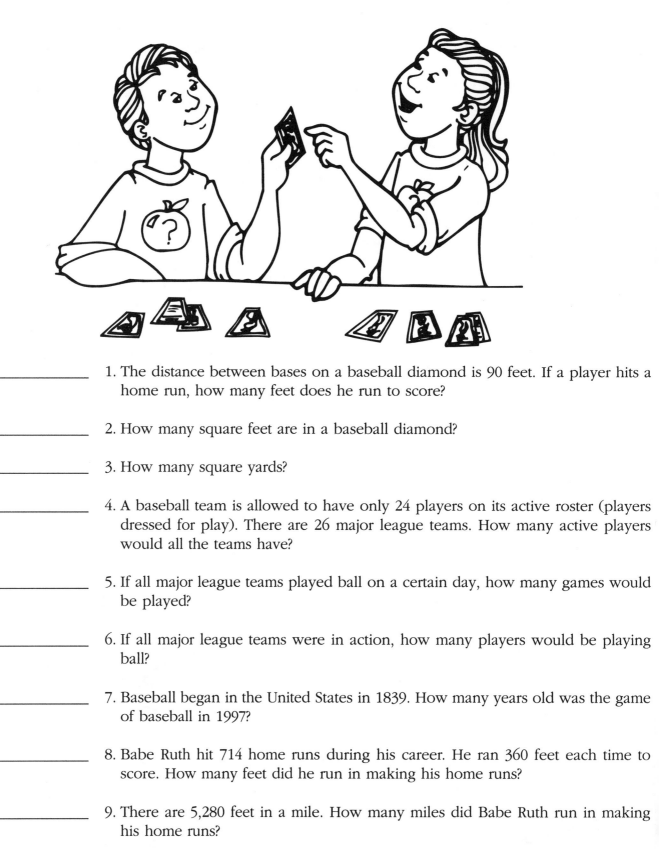

_____ 1. The distance between bases on a baseball diamond is 90 feet. If a player hits a home run, how many feet does he run to score?

_____ 2. How many square feet are in a baseball diamond?

_____ 3. How many square yards?

_____ 4. A baseball team is allowed to have only 24 players on its active roster (players dressed for play). There are 26 major league teams. How many active players would all the teams have?

_____ 5. If all major league teams played ball on a certain day, how many games would be played?

_____ 6. If all major league teams were in action, how many players would be playing ball?

_____ 7. Baseball began in the United States in 1839. How many years old was the game of baseball in 1997?

_____ 8. Babe Ruth hit 714 home runs during his career. He ran 360 feet each time to score. How many feet did he run in making his home runs?

_____ 9. There are 5,280 feet in a mile. How many miles did Babe Ruth run in making his home runs?

32

GA1610 Good Apple © 1997

Spring Sports Facts

Fill in the missing numbers in each paragraph. Be sure to use numbers that fit the facts given in each case.

1. The city soccer league raised $500 for new T-shirts by selling pizzas. It sold _____ large pizzas at $3.00 a piece. It sold an equal amount of small pizzas for _____ dollars each. The local sports shop sold the T-shirts imprinted with the team names for the special price of $5.99. The soccer league was able to purchase _____ T-shirts with the profit remaining after paying the pizza distributor $1.00 a piece for the 200 pizzas sold.

2. The Hilldale Junior High four-man relay team competed in a medley-relay race. In a medley-relay race, each member must use a different stroke. The swimmer using the crawl swam _____ meters. The swimmer using the backstroke swam half the distance for a total of _____ meters. The swimmer using the breaststroke gained 20 meters more than the second swimmer for a total of 60 meters. The swimmer using the butterfly stroke swam _____ meters—twice the distance of the swimmer using the crawl. All total, the team swam a distance of _____ meters.

3. One-third of the 29,556 fans attending the opening baseball game of the season had reserved seats. The remaining _____ fans sat in the bleachers. The stadium sold one-half of the reserved-seat tickets at the adult price of $7.00 each and an equal number at the children's price of _____ dollars and _____ cents. The reserved-seat gate netted the stadium $51,723. Ticket sales for bleacher seats brought in an additional $44,334 for _____ adult ticket prices of _____ dollars each and an equal number of children's half-price tickets at $1.50 each.

Sports Math

All sports events boil down to the final score, which is based on numbers. Score points in this game by providing the correct numbers below.

_____ 1. A basketball court is 94 feet long. How many yards is it?

_____ 2. A football field is 100 yards long. If a quarterback can pass the ball 100 feet, how may passes will it take to cover the length of the field?

_____ 3. During one soccer game, Team A was awarded 5 penalty kicks. Penalty kicks are taken 12 yards from the goal. If the soccer ball made it to the goal all 5 times, how many inches did it travel?

_____ 4. A runner's time was 10 seconds for 100 yards. How many feet per second did he cover?

_____ 5. A professional basketball team played 82 games and won the league with 62 victories. What was its winning percentage?

_____ 6. There are 18 holes on a golf course. If the golf course is 7,000 yards, what is the average yardage per hole? (Round to the nearest tenth.)

_____ 7. Michael Jordan makes 8 of 12 field goals and 10 of 14 free throws. How many points does he score?

_____ 8. Elaine is running 5,000 meters, and Holly is running 2 miles. Which one is running the greater distance?

_____ 9. Cher is running in the 880-yard race, and Linda is running a mile. Who is running the greater distance?

_____ 10. The Kentucky Derby is 1 1/4 miles. A horse wins the race in 2 minutes. How many miles per hour was the horse going?

GA1610 Good Apple © 1997

Sports Math

_____ 11. A golf foursome (4 players) shoots scores of 68, 70, 76, 73. Par is 72. Did the foursome average over or under par?

_____ 12. Noel has 14 hits in 42 at bats. What is the batting average?

_____ 13. Nathan hits 8 of 18 shots in a basketball game. What is his field goal percentage?

_____ 14. Brandon has shot 120 free throws. He is hitting an excellent 90%. How many has he hit?

_____ 15. Tim has a fabulous day at bat hitting a single, double, triple, and home run. How many total bases did he have?

_____ 16. The Indianapolis 500 is a race of 500 miles. If the winning driver averages 125 miles per hour, how long does it take to run the race?

_____ 17. A football team scores every possible way in a game: A touchdown (6 points), point after (1), field goal (3), safety (2). Do they beat a team that scores 5 field goals?

_____ 18. In golf, a bogie is one over par, and a birdie is one under par. If par for 18 holes is 72 and a player shoots 7 bogies, 5 birdies, and 6 pars, what is his score?

_____ 19. In an airplane race, if a plane flies at Mach I (750 miles per hour), how long will it take to go 3,000 miles?

_____ 20. If it goes Mach II (1,500 miles per hour), how long will it take to go around the world (approximately 25,000 miles)?
(Round to the nearest tenth.)

Football Pass

You will need to keep your eye on the ball and your mind on your math as you figure out these football word problems. Use the special football field number line to help you. A knowledge of negative and positive numbers and absolute value is a plus, but is not necessary if you can make good use of the number line and your addition and subtraction skills. Keep track of where the ball is in the blanks after each step. Be sure to include whose side of the field each team is on.

Spartans   **Wildcats**

0 5 10 15 20 25 30 35 40 45 50 45 40 35 30 25 20 15 10 5 0

1. A - The Spartans kick off 52 yards from their 35-yard line.   _____
   B - The Wildcats run 18 yards with the ball.   _____
   C - The Wildcats lose 6 yards on the next play.   _____
   D - The Wildcats complete a 21-yard pass.   _____
   E - They run for 9 yards on the following play.   _____

What yard line are the Wildcats on now? _____

2. A - The Wildcats punt from their 39-yard line. It's a 44-yard kick. _____
   B - After a fair catch, the Spartans lose 2 yards on the next play. _____
   C - The Spartans complete a 26-yard pass on the next play.   _____
   D - They complete a 16-yard pass on the following play.   _____
   E - Then they lose 7 yards on the next play.   _____

Where are the Spartans now? _____

3. A - Spartans are at their own 43-yard line.   _____
   B - They throw an 18-yard pass which is intercepted by the Wildcats. _____
   C - The Wildcats run 6 yards with the intercepted pass.   _____
   D - They run 12 yards on the following play.   _____
   E - Next, the Wildcats complete a 15-yard pass.   _____

Where are the Wildcats now? _____

4. A - The Spartans complete a 9-yard pass from their own 49-yard line. _____
   B - They run 7 yards on the next play.   _____
   C - They lose 2 yards next.   _____
   D - Then they complete a 9-yard pass.   _____
   E - Finally, they complete a 28-yard pass.   _____

Where are they now and what happened? _____

GA1610 Good Apple © 1997

It's Baseball Time Again

How do you know which baseball team is in first place? What is your batting average? Has it improved from last year? The exercises below will help you find percentages which can be used to answer the questions above.

Below is a list of baseball teams and the number of games each has won and lost. Compute the percentage of games won by each team. Then place a "1" in the standing blank for the team in first place, a "2" for the team in second place, and so on.

Team	Won	Lost	Winning Percentage	Standing
Tigers	12	4	_____	_____
Lions	5	11	_____	_____
Leopards	7	9	_____	_____
Mice	11	5	_____	_____
Rats	13	3	_____	_____
Monkeys	6	10	_____	_____
Moose	2	14	_____	_____
Deer	8	8	_____	_____

The number of times that certain people batted, the hits, and the walks are listed below. Find the hitting percentage for each player. Remember that walks are not counted in finding the hitting percentage. In the blank marked "Standing," place a number "1" for the best hitter, a "2" for the second best, and so on.

Player	Bats	Hits	Walks	Batting Percentage	Standing
Tom	42	12	3	_____	_____
Mary	41	9	2	_____	_____
Sam	47	14	2	_____	_____
Dotti	44	11	4	_____	_____
Mike	40	16	2	_____	_____
Kim	27	7	0	_____	_____
Tom	23	7	2	_____	_____
Angie	31	9	5	_____	_____
John	38	14	4	_____	_____
Patti	49	18	1	_____	_____

Up to Bat

No special knowledge of mathematics is needed to solve this word problem, but you will need to use your analysis, deductive reasoning, and sequencing skills.

In this exercise, you will need to match the batting averages given with the names of the 9 starting players. Using the grid should help. To fill it in, put an "X" in each square where you have eliminated a possibility. Once you have eliminated all but 1 possibility for a given row or column, draw a baseball in that square to show that a particular name and batting average go together. When you have completed the grid, answer the question at the bottom of the page.

1. Neither the highest nor the lowest average belongs to a boy.
2. Ed has the medium average.
3. Isaac's average is less than Carl's but more than Ed's.
4. Carl and Felicia have the averages closest to Isaac.
5. Helen has the second to the lowest average.
6. Betsy's average is higher than Greg's average which is higher than Albert's average.

	.500	.450	.425	.400	.375	.350	.325	.300	.275
Albert									
Betsy									
Carl									
Diane									
Ed									
Felicia									
Greg									
Helen									
Isaac									

What was each player's batting average?

Albert _____   Diane _____   Greg _____

Betsy _____   Ed _____   Helen _____

Carl _____   Felicia _____   Isaac _____

GA1610 Good Apple © 1997

Par for the Course

The information given below tells how one player scored on each hole of a golf course. Use the given information to answer the questions. Trial and error will work in figuring out the answers, but it is best to set up this problem algebraically.

1. The player scored par on Hole #3.
2. He scored three more on Hole #7 than on Hole #3.
3. He scored one less on Hole #4 than on Hole #3.
4. The score on Hole #5 was twice the score of Hole #4.
5. The score on Hole #2 was half the score of Hole #3.
6. The player scored a seven on Hole #6.
7. The score for Hole #9 was one more than the score for Hole #3.
8. The score on Hole #1 was four times the score of Hole #2.
9. The score on Hole #8 was the same as the score on Hole #6 minus Hole #3.
10. The average for the nine holes was scored on Hole #9.
11. The player shot a nine over par for the whole course.

What was the player's score for each hole?

Hole #1 _____   Hole #2 _____   Hole #3 _____

Hole #4 _____   Hole #5 _____   Hole #6 _____

Hole #7 _____   Hole #8 _____   Hole #9 _____

What was the player's total score for all nine holes? _____

What was the par for the whole course? _____

All Sports Math

_____ 1. A professional golfer entered 30 tournaments in one year and won $490,000. What were his average earnings per tournament? (Round to the nearest dollar.)

_____ 2. A famous baseball player sells his autograph for $8.00. If he writes his name in 5 seconds, how much money does he make in a two-hour autograph session?

_____ 3. A star basketball player hit 48% of his shots. If he attempted 400 shots, how many baskets did he make?

_____ 4. A professional baseball player was at bat 600 times during a season. His batting average was .280. How many hits did he have?

_____ 5. There are 10 minutes and 47 seconds left in a basketball game. How many total seconds are left in the game?

_____ 6. A baseball pitcher has an ERA (earned run average) of 3.70 a game. If he pitches 27 complete games, how many runs does he allow?

_____ 7. A football player averaged 120.5 yards a game. How many feet did he gain in a 14-game season?

_____ 8. The starting 11 players for a football team average 225 pounds. What is the weight of the entire starting team?

_____ 9. A fishing party caught 34 fish weighing a total of 168 pounds. What was the average weight per fish? (Round to the nearest one-hundredth.)

_____ 10. A horse farm owner sells 24 racehorses for $1,048,000. What is the average price per horse?

GA1610 Good Apple © 1997

All Sports Math

continued

_____ 11. A batter had 2 hits in 6 times at bat. What was his average for the day?

_____ 12. A ski resort receives 240 inches of snow in a season. It takes 10 inches of snow to equal 1 inch of rain. How many inches of rain would the 240 inches of snow equal?

_____ 13. Last year, one state had 25,000 acres of forest burn. Human carelessness caused 80% of the damage. How much damage was due to natural causes?

_____ 14. It costs $3.00 to enter a fishing derby that has prizes totaling $44,000. How many tickets must be sold for the sponsors to break even?

_____ 15. Three regions within a state have a total of 317 eagles. If region 1 has 84 eagles and region 2 has 27 eagles, how many eagles are in region 3?

_____ 16. A horse race awarded prize money totaling $4,000. The first-place winner received 50%, the second-place winner received 30%, and the third-place winner received 20%. How much money did each winner receive?

_____ 17. A big game hunters' banquet costs $15 per person, or $25 a couple. How much can 12 people save if they go as couples?

_____ 18. During a period of one year 2,000,000 duck stamps were sold in the United States at $10 a stamp. The money was to be used to buy wetlands. How many acres of wetlands could be purchased from the proceeds at a cost of $1,200 an acre?

_____ 19. A football team won 3 games by an average of 13 points. They won game 1 by 1 point, game 2 by 7 points. What was the winning margin for game 3?

_____ 20. A basketball player averaged 13 points and 5.6 rebounds per game. How many points and rebounds did he have in a 30-game season?

Finding Areas

To solve the problems in this unit, you will need to find the areas of circles, squares, triangles, rectangles, and parallelograms. A drawing of each figure is given below with parts labeled and named. Study the figures and become familiar with the terms.

The formula for finding the area of each particular figure is given. Study the formulas. Remember them for future math.

All area answers should be given in square units (inches, feet, yards).

In this unit, the Greek letter π (pi) equals 3.14.

In this unit, there can be more than one way to find solutions to some problems.

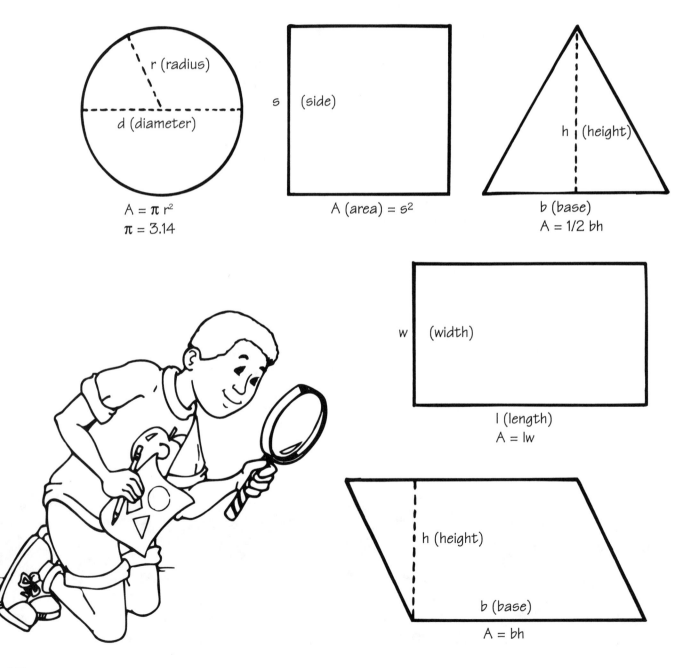

$A = \pi r^2$
$\pi = 3.14$

$A \text{ (area)} = s^2$

$A = 1/2\,bh$

$A = lw$

$A = bh$

Finding Areas I

Find the area of each shaded part.

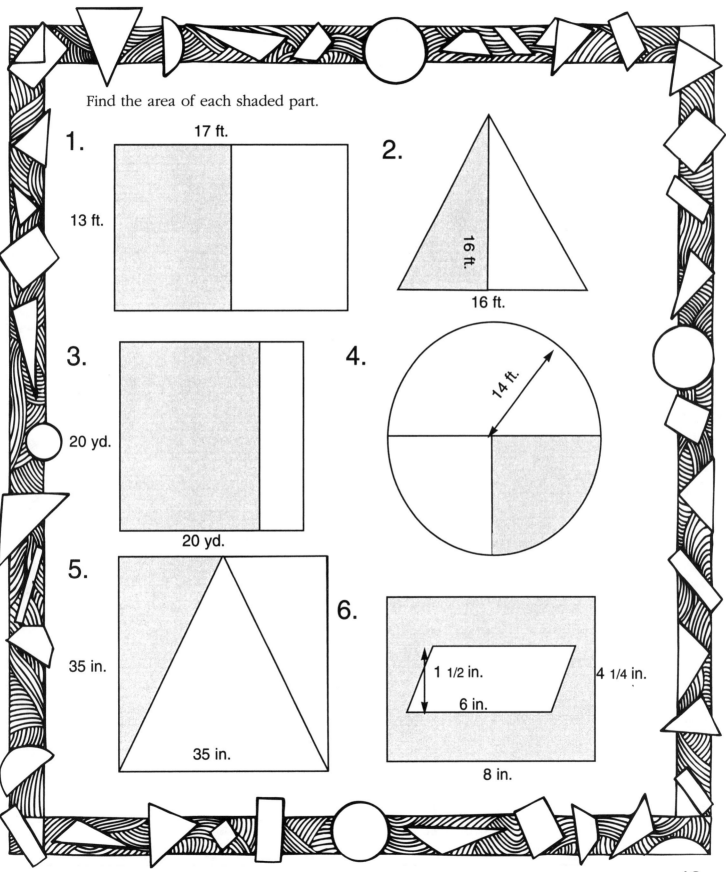

1. 17 ft. / 13 ft.

2. 16 ft. / 16 ft.

3. 20 yd. / 20 yd.

4. 14 ft.

5. 35 in. / 35 in.

6. 1 1/2 in. / 6 in. / 4 1/4 in. / 8 in.

Finding Areas II

Find the area of each unshaded part.

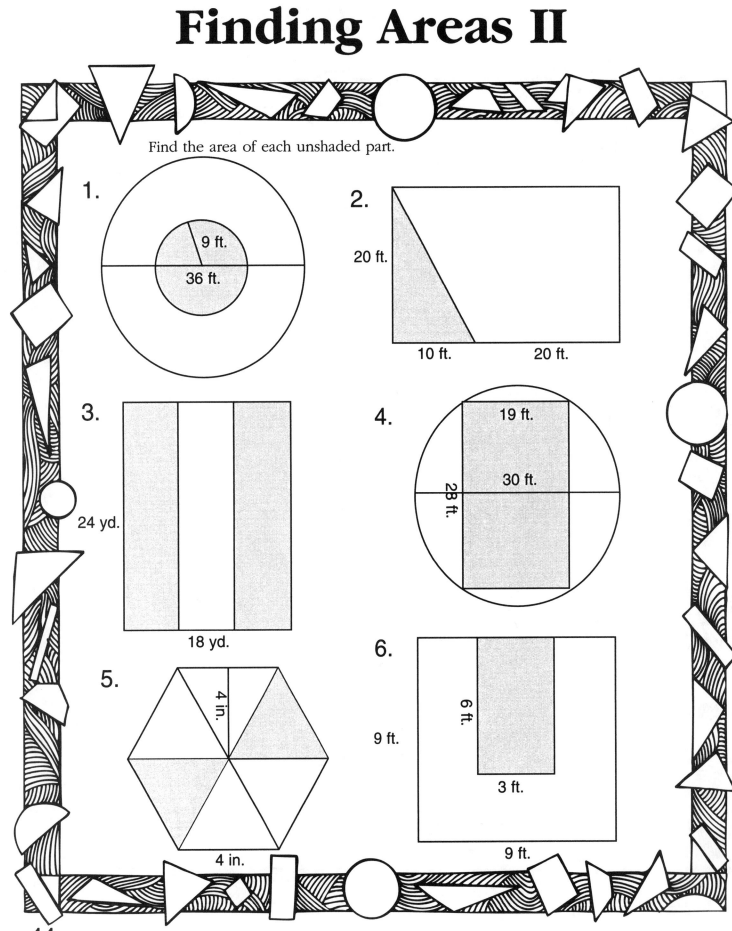

1.

9 ft.

36 ft.

2.

20 ft.

10 ft.   20 ft.

3.

24 yd.

18 yd.

4.

19 ft.

30 ft.

28 ft.

5.

4 in.

4 in.

6.

6 ft.

9 ft.

3 ft.

9 ft.

44

Finding the Areas of Polygons

Find the area of each figure below. Count each full square as one. Place the number of squares in the correct spaces at the right. Remember, additional lines can be drawn outside the figures to form a polygon whose area is easy to calculate (a triangle can be made into a square and then you find the area of the square and divide it by two).

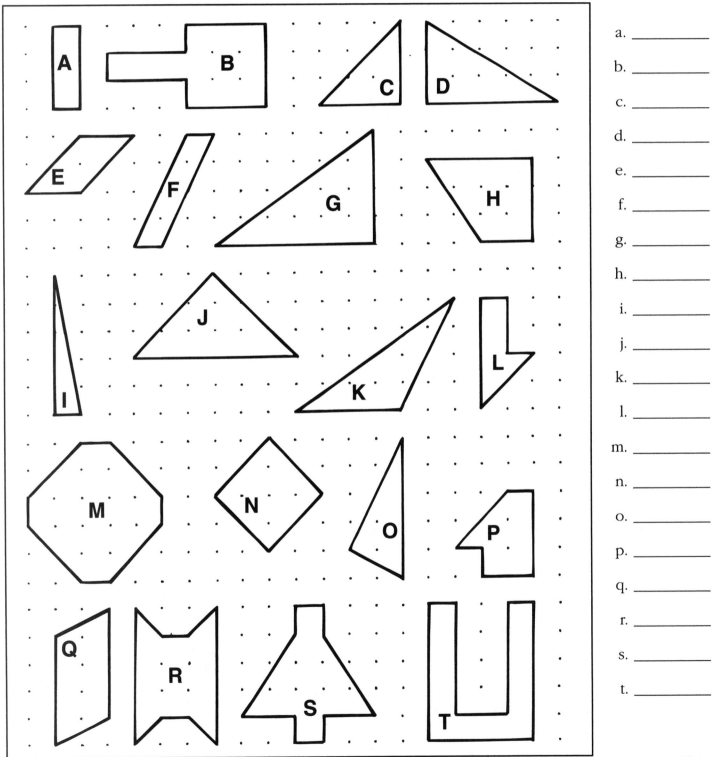

a. _____

b. _____

c. _____

d. _____

e. _____

f. _____

g. _____

h. _____

i. _____

j. _____

k. _____

l. _____

m. _____

n. _____

o. _____

p. _____

q. _____

r. _____

s. _____

t. _____

Triangular Spectacular

Which figures below will the triangles to the right form? All the triangles must be used!

Line Designs

Which designs below can be formed by using exactly 10 equal lines? List them by number.

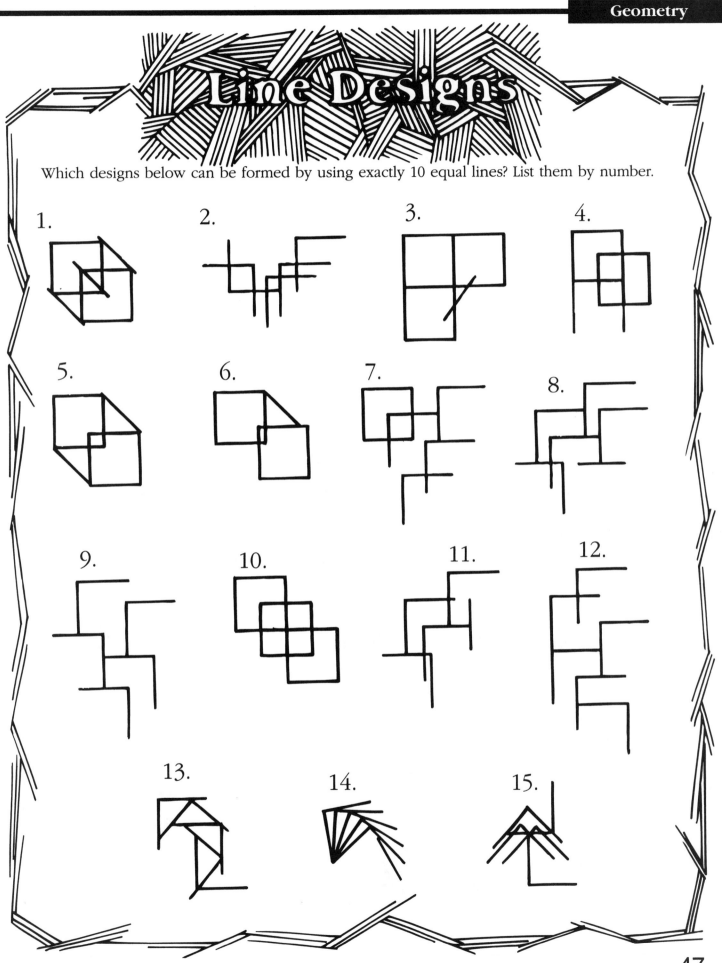

1.

2.

3.

4.

5.

6.

7.

8.

9.

10.

11.

12.

13.

14.

15.

GA1610 Good Apple © 1997

Geopuzzle

Geometry can be a lot of fun. Test your skills with the following activity.

1. Cut out the geometric puzzle pieces below and match them to their geometric figures on page 49. (Notice that the puzzle pieces of each figure are congruent parts.)
2. Identify the geometric figures.
3. Draw a line of symmetry between the congruent pieces on each geometric figure.
4. As an extra challenge, write the total number of degrees of the interior angles of each geometric figure. (Hint: Count the number of triangles in each figure. Remember, a triangle contains 180°.)

GA1610 Good Apple © 1997

Geopuzzle

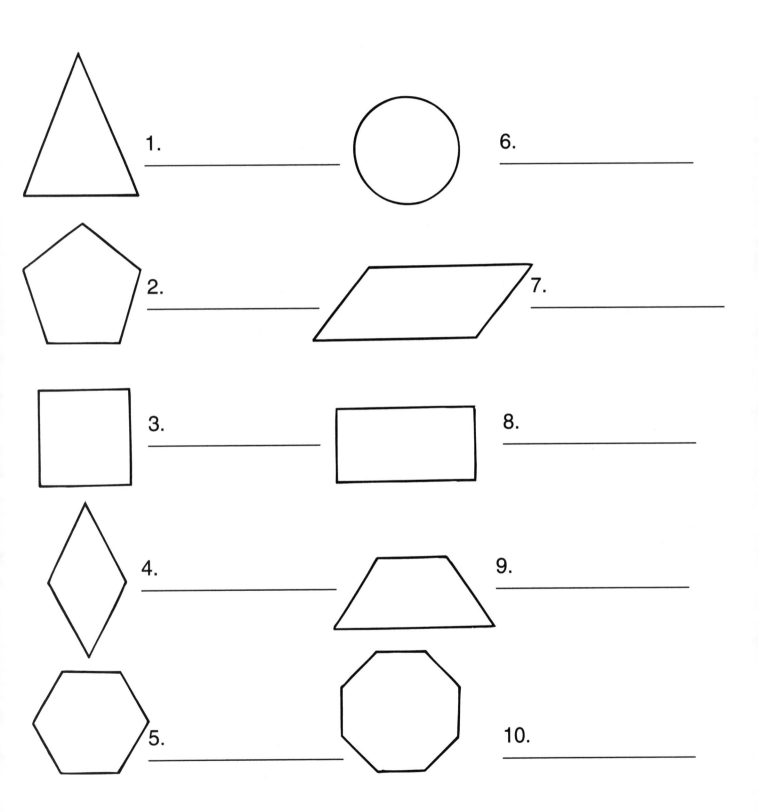

1. _____

2. _____

3. _____

4. _____

5. _____

6. _____

7. _____

8. _____

9. _____

10. _____

Shaping Up

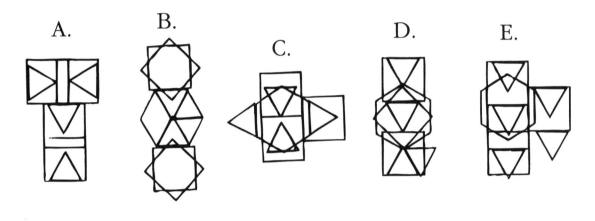

Can you find the five designs below that can be formed using all of the shapes above?

A. B. C. D. E.

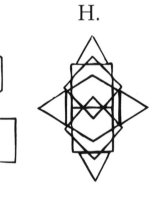

F. G. H. I. J.

K. L. M. N. O.

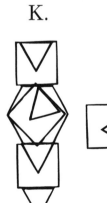

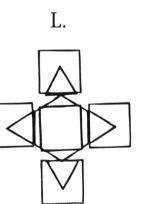

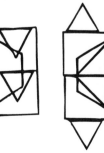

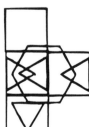

Geometric Match-Up

Twenty-five geometrical terms are listed on the left. On the right is a drawing of each. Match correct pairs. Write the letter of the correct illustration on the line in front of the term.

_____ 1. line

_____ 2. ray

_____ 3. isosceles triangle

_____ 4. trapezoid

_____ 5. arc

_____ 6. circle

_____ 7. parallel lines

_____ 8. square

_____ 9. rectangle

_____ 10. diameter (of a circle)

_____ 11. pentagon

_____ 12. hexagon

_____ 13. semicircle

_____ 14. radius (of a circle)

_____ 15. ellipse

_____ 16. perpendicular lines

_____ 17. line segment

_____ 18. right triangle

_____ 19. scalene triangle

_____ 20. acute angle

_____ 21. obtuse angle

_____ 22. equilateral triangle

_____ 23. central angle

_____ 24. complementary angles

_____ 25. supplementary angles

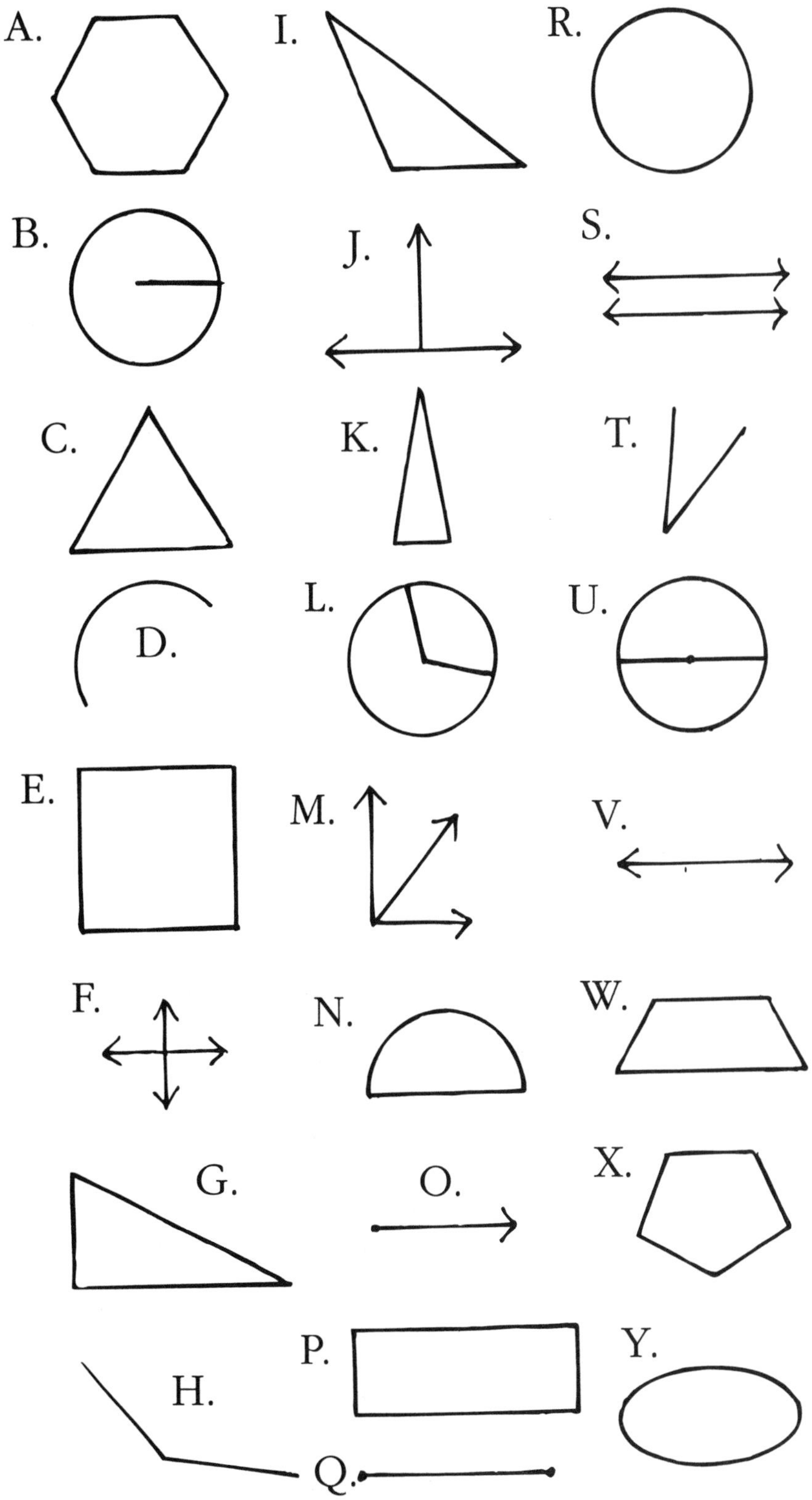

Geometric Bubblegram

Write the word that fits each definition below. Place one letter on each line and in each bubble to solve the message in the bubblegram.

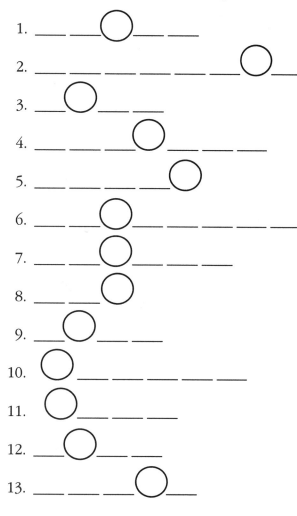

1. Formed by two rays with a common end point.
2. Kinds of planes that do not intersect.
3. A geometric figure with one circular base.
4. A part of a line with two end points.
5. A set of points on a flat surface.
6. The point where lines meet.
7. A curve with all its points the same distance from the center.
8. A part of a line with one end point.
9. A straight curve with no end points.
10. A flat figure with four equal sides and four right angles.
11. The surface of a geometric figure.
12. A geometric figure with six square faces.
13. The intersection of a line and a plane.

What is the message in the bubblegram?

_____ ____ ____ ____ ____ ____   ____ ____ ____ ____ ____ ____ ____ ____!

52

The Shapes of Our Lives

Geometric shapes are everywhere! They are indeed a part of our everyday lives. We eat them; we live in them; we obey the symbolism they represent; we use them as tools to make our work easier; we use them during play; and we even visit them on vacation. When you really stop and think about it, the whole world and most all that we do in it is pretty much related to shapes. Below are some exercises that will get your mind into "shape," too. Read each clue, then decide what the mystery object is. Jot it down and place the name we use to represent that shape there, too.

1. The symbol forces us to stop what we've already started.

2. We could visit these ancient burial sites so far away if only we had the funds.

3. We shoot them into little holes across a field of green felt.

4. They're fun to fix and fun to eat. We load them up with cheese and sausage and mushrooms and other good things to eat.

5. Some are grass and some aren't, but they all serve as battlefields for the likes of the Bears, the Lions, the Bengals, and others.

6. Top-level decisions concerning the security of our nation are made here.

7. The warmth provided by this old friend makes it possible for us to live here on the planet Earth.

8. The distance from home to first and to third is much the same, but from home to second is quite another matter.

9. For pies and play and other things, too, it "rolls out the dough."

10. A percussion of silver that rings in our ears whenever struck by another piece of silver.

11. They're sweet to the taste and fattening, too, except for the middle, which is nothing but air.

12. We spend about a third of our lives here preparing to meet the other two-thirds.

13. We communicate thoughts from our minds to paper through the use of these.

14. Through these we find our futures as well as what's on the other side.

Now that you have that mind "in shape," think of some other shapes that are a part of our everyday lives. Jot them down and figure out clues that will challenge your classmates and "shape up" their thinking, too!

Geometry Crossword Puzzle

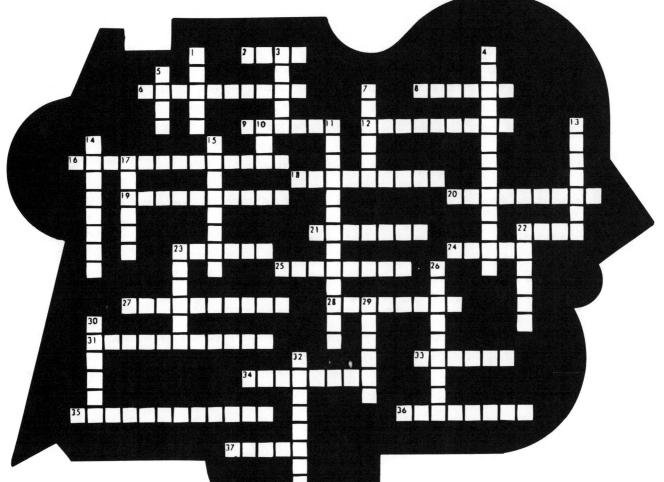

Across

2. The line or plane upon which a figure is thought of as resting
6. Having 4 sides and 4 angles
8. Four equal sides
9. Distance to the center of a circle
12. A polygon in which only opposite sides are equal in length with 4 right angles
16. Distance around a circle
18. A plane figure with 4 sides; 2 of which are parallel
19. Half of a straight angle
20. A triangle with 2 equal sides
21. An equilateral parallelogram that does not have right angles
22. The path of a moving point, having length but not breadth
23. Space inside a figure
24. Flat surfaces
25. Lines that never meet or cross
27. An angle more than zero degrees and less than 90 degrees
28. The branch of mathematics that deals with lines, points, surfaces, and other properties of space
31. An angle more than 180 degrees and less than 360 degrees
33. The distance from the base to the top
34. Closed plane figures formed by joining 3 or more straight lines and angles
35. Straight lines crossing over each other
36. Opposite of horizontal
37. A straight line joining any 2 points on an arc, curve, or circle

Down

1. Measurement of the extent of something from side to side
3. Geometry dealing with 3-dimensional figures
4. A figure with 4 sides; the opposite sides are equal and parallel
5. An object which has length, width, and height
7. A plane curve with each point on the curve being equidistant from a fixed point at the center of the figure
10. A portion of a circle going from one point to another
11. A straight line
13. A 3-sided figure with no sides equal in length
14. Distance across a circle
15. A figure with 3 sides
17. A line that bends continuously, not a line that is straight or broken
22. Measurement of the extent of an object along its greatest dimension
23. The point of intersection of two sides of an angle
26. Distance around the outside of a circle
29. An angle more than 90 degrees and less than 180 degrees
30. A line with angles; not straight
32. A solid figure with the ends being equal and parallel circles

54

Little Insects—Big Numbers

Insects are small, but there are so many of them (probably over 2 billion species with several billions of individuals in many species) that they offer strong competition to humans for food. All over the world there are some insects that cause crop damage and carry diseases. Overall, however, the number of harmful insects is small. Most are helpful in pollinating plants and producing food and other useful products.

_____ 1. The largest ants are about 1 inch long. The average human is about 5 feet 9 inches tall. How many ants would it take to equal one average human?

_____ 2. The smallest ant colonies may have about 10 ants, the largest 500,000. How many small ant colonies would it take to equal the largest colony?

_____ 3. A male ant may live only 5 weeks, but a queen may live 15 years. How many weeks longer does a queen live than a male?

_____ 4. If an army ant queen lays 30,000 eggs every 6 weeks, how many will she lay in 10 years? (Round to the nearest whole number of weeks in a 10-year period.)

_____ 5. The cost of keeping harmful insects in check in the United States is over $1,600,000,000 yearly. If the boll weevil costs $200,000,000, what percentage is that of the total?

_____ 6. If clothes moths do $22,000,000 worth of damage annually, what percentage is that of the $1,750,000,000 spent on clothes annually in the country?

_____ 7. If there are 800,000 species of insects and only 0.1% are harmful, what is the number of harmful species?

_____ 8. Midges are about 1/20 of an inch long. One of the largest flies is about 3 inches long. How many times longer is the fly that the midge?

_____ 9. Some midges move their wings 1,000 times a second. A housefly beats its wings 200 times a second. How many times slower does the housefly's wings beat than the midge's?

_____ 10. The population of the United States is about 250,000,000. A housefly lays 1,000 eggs during her lifetime. How many female houseflies would it take to match the population of the United States if (horrors) all the eggs hatched and lived?

Little Insects—Big Numbers

_____11. The population of the world is about 5,000,000,000. How many female flies would it take to match the population of the world?

_____12. There are 2,000 kinds of mosquitoes in the world, and 150 live in the United States. What percentage of all mosquitoes live in the United States?

_____13. If a male mosquito lives 20 days and is deaf for the first 48 hours of its life, what percentage of its life is it deaf?

_____14. If a fly lays 1,000 eggs in a lifetime and a mosquito 3,000, how many flies would it take to lay 1,200,000 eggs? How many mosquitoes?

_____15. If 250 harmful insects in the United States are only one twenty-fifth of one percent, how many species (kinds) of insects are in the United States?

_____16. If a male mosquito lives 20 days and a female 30 days, how many more hours does a female live than a male?

_____17. If a mayfly lives only one day, how many seconds does it live?

_____18. A mayfly has one of the shortest life spans at one day. Some turtles have the longest at 150 years (365 days = 1 year). How many more days does the turtle live than the mayfly?

_____19. Some spiders like to eat insects. If there are 30,000 species of spiders and 900,000 species of insects, how many species of insects would there be for each species of spider to eat?

_____20. The smallest mosquito is 1/16 of an inch, the largest 5/8 of an inch. How many small mosquitoes would it take to make one large one?

GA1610 Good Apple © 1997

Environmental Numbers

_____ 1. It is estimated there are 23,500,000 deer in the United States, more than there were before Columbus discovered America. In 1900 there were about 500,000. About how many times has the deer population increased since 1900?

_____ 2. About 12,200,000 deer hunters spent $6,000,000,000 on the sport. What is the average cost per hunter?

_____ 3. Sizeable populations of white-tailed deer are found in 47 of the 50 states. What percent of states do not have white-tailed deer?

_____ 4. In 1934, 35 deer were turned loose in Indiana. In 1993 there were 175,000. What was the average growth per year?

_____ 5. Michigan has 1,500,000 white-tailed deer and 9,240,000 people. About how many people are there for each deer?

_____ 6. Texas has 3,700,000 white-tailed deer, Michigan 1,500,000, Alabama 1,300,000, and Georgia 1,200,000. If there are 23,500,000 in the United States, how many deer are in the other 46 states?

_____ 7. Key deer weigh only 55 pounds while big bucks reach 400 pounds. About how many key deer would it take to equal one large buck?

_____ 8. Michigan's deer population of 1,500,000 is 200,000 more than it should be. What is the percent of overpopulation?

_____ 9. Many animals and plants are facing extinction due to the destruction of rain forests. It is estimated 20 to 50 million acres are destroyed each year. If 37 million acres are destroyed in a year and 12 million acres are destroyed by logging, what percent is destroyed for other purposes? (Round to the nearest tenth.)

Environmental Numbers

_____ 10. Destroying rain forests causes an estimated 100 plant and animal species to become extinct each day. How many plants and animals will become extinct in a year?

_____ 11. The tallest trees may be 150 feet high. If a one-story building is 10 feet tall, how many stories would the tallest trees equal?

_____ 12. There are about 10 million species of plants and animals in the world. Of these, 7 million live in the rain forest. What percent live outside the rain forest?

_____ 13. Over the last 35 years, 50% of 215 million acres of wetlands have been destroyed. How many acres have been lost? What is the average number of acres lost per year?

_____ 14. There are 6,000 landfills in operation in the United States. One-third are expected to be full in the next five years. How many landfills will be left?

_____ 15. The National Audubon Society's 89th bird tally involved 1,500 groups made up of 41,000 volunteers. What was the average group size?

_____ 16. One group on Lake Erie counted 32,888 birds of 68 species. If all species had equal numbers, what would have been the average number per species?

_____ 17. Disposable diapers make up 2% of landfill waste. If there are 6,000 landfills, how many would disposable diapers fill?

GA1610 Good Apple © 1997

Solar System Numbers

The solar system affects us every minute of our lives. The way we count time is based on the solar system. The seasons and the clothes we wear, our vacations, the crops that are grown, and the food we eat are all directly from Earth and its relationship to the sun. Figure out some of the more common aspects of the solar system in the following problems.

1. The Islamic year is 1410 and the Chinese year is 4626. Is the Chinese year greater in number than the U.S. and Islamic years combined?

2. When Earth is at aphelion (farthest distance from sun), it is 94,512,258 miles from the sun. When it is at perihelion (closest distance to sun), it is 91,400,005 miles from the sun.
   a) What is the difference?
   b) What is the average?

3. There are several principal meteor showers that can be seen at certain times of the year. The original showers can be seen at a rate of 10 to 70 per hour. If you watched the showers for 6 hours, how many meteors would you see. . .
   a) at minimum?
   b) at maximum?

4. What percent is the minimum rate of the maximum rate?

5. The Quadrantid meteor shower has the greatest meteor display at a rate of 40 to 150 per hour, and the Taurid meteor shower has the smallest at 5 to 15.
   a) Figure the average of both meteor showers.
   b) Taking the average, how many more meteors would you see in 5 hours by watching the Quadrantids?

6. The star Algol has a magnitude of 2.2, and Betelgeuse has a magnitude of 0.7. Approximately how many times greater is Algol than Betelgeuse?

7. In 1988, Earth was close to Mars (36,300,000 miles away). The moon is about 240,000 miles from Earth. How much farther from Earth is Mars than the moon?

Solar System Numbers

continued

8. If Mars was 36,300,000 miles from Earth in 1988, how many hours would it take a rocket traveling 2,000 miles an hour to reach Mars?

9. On Christmas Day, the sun rises in New York City at 7:18 a.m. and sets at 4:34 p.m. How long is the day?

10. Over a 6-year span, there are 3 years with 12 full moons and 3 years with 13 full moons.
    a) What is the average number of full moons for the 6 years?
    b) What is the total for 6 years?

11. Some volcanoes on Mars are 70,000 feet high.
    a) How many yards is that (to the nearest yard)?
    b) How many miles is that (to the nearest mile)?

12. Our solar system is part of the galaxy we call the Milky Way. There are about 100 billion stars in the Milky Way. About one out of 1,000 stars have planets and smaller bodies circling them. How many stars in the Milky Way have planets?

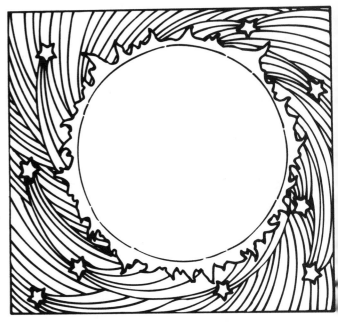

13. The sun spins around the center of the Milky Way at 175 miles per second.
    a) How many miles does it cover in one minute?
    b) How many miles does it cover in one hour?

14. It takes the whole solar system over 200 years to make one revolution around the center of the Milky Way. If Earth is 4 billion years old, how many revolutions has our solar system made?

15. The amount of time it takes to orbit the sun is called a year. Earth has a year of 365.26 days. Mercury's year is 88 days, and Pluto's is 247.7 days.
    a) About how many times longer is Earth's year than Mercury's?
    b) How much longer is Pluto's year than Mercury's?

16. On Earth, a baseball player can throw a ball 280 feet. On Mars, he can throw it 3 times as far as he can on Earth, but on Jupiter he can throw it 2/5 as far.
    a) How far can he throw a ball on Mars?
    b) How far can he throw it on Jupiter?

60

The Cost of Pollution

_____ 1. An Exxon tanker ran aground and spilled 240,000 barrels of crude oil in the harbor of Valdez, Alaska. If there are 50 gallons in a barrel, how many gallons were spilled?

_____ 2. The price of gasoline increased 15 cents a gallon after the accident in Alaska. If 125,000,000 gallons of gasoline are used in the United States each day, what was the total cost of the accident per day to consumers?

_____ 3. How much did the increase cost drivers in the U.S. for March? April?

_____ 4. The Environmental Protection Agency reported 22,000,000,000 pounds of chemicals were released in the air during 1987. If there are 250,000,000 people in the United States, how many pounds was that for each person?

_____ 5. One industrial state sent 158,400,000 pounds in the air during 1987. With a population of 9,000,000 how many pounds was that for each person?

_____ 6. The top 5 states in air pollution released in pounds: 239,000; 173,000; 138,000; 135,000; and 132,000. What was the total for these states?

_____ 7. The top 5 states in water pollution released in pounds: 3,835,000,000; 774,000,000; 659,000,000; 605,000,000; and 474,000,000. How many pounds of water pollution were released?

_____ 8. The top 5 states in land pollution released in pounds: 835,000,000; 247,000,000; 191,000,000; 165,000,000; and 156,000,000. What was the combined total of pounds for air, waste, and land pollution?

_____ 9. One state which produced 8,000,000 pounds of hazardous waste disposed of only 1,500,000 pounds in hazardous waste facilities. What percentage was this?

_____ 10. The EPA states that each person in the United States generates 3.5 pounds of garbage a day. How many pounds is that for a population of 250,000,000?

continued

The Cost of Pollution

_____ 11. If 33% of the garbage was recycled, how many pounds would that be?

_____ 12. If 500,000 trees are used in the United States for the Sunday editions of newspapers, how many trees will be used in a year for these editions?

_____ 13. If 2,500,000 plastic bottles are disposed of each hour, how many will be thrown away in 24 hours?

_____ 14. How many plastic bottles will be disposed of in January?

_____ 15. If one quart of oil can contaminate 2 acres of water, how many acres could 240,000 barrels (50 gallons per barrel) spilled from an Alaskan tanker contaminate if nothing was done to clean up the spill?

_____ 16. If 50% of the paper from Sunday editions of newspapers was recycled (see number 2), how many trees could be saved in October?

_____ 17. If the United States uses 6,400,000,000 barrels of oil a year, how many barrels is that per day?

_____ 18. If the average gasoline consumption per car is 20 miles per gallon, how many miles can be driven using 200 barrels?

_____ 19. If the average driver uses 10 gallons of gasoline per week, how many gallons will he or she use in 40 years of driving?

_____ 20. If the driver paid an average of $1 per gallon, how much would he or she pay for 10 gallons a week for 50 years?

62

Space Figures

The space program depends on exact mathematics. Some of the figures are enormous. See if you could become a member of the space program by answering these problems.

_____ 1. A space station will cost $23,000,000,000. If $900,000,000 is spent each year, how long will it be before the station is paid for (to the nearest year)?

_____ 2. A manned space flight costs $300,000,000. An unmanned flight costs $50,000,000. How many times more does a manned flight cost than an unmanned flight?

_____ 3. After the *Challenger* exploded in January 1986 killing its crew of 7, there were 56 major design changes and 400 minor changes to make the shuttle safer. These changes cost $2,400,000,000. What was the average cost of each change?

_____ 4. The circumference of Earth is about 25,000 miles. The space shuttle *Discovery* went around Earth 64 times. How many miles did it go?

_____ 5. Thirty-two months separated the *Challenger*'s explosion and the *Discovery*'s mission. Of the $2,400,000,000 spent on design changes during this time, what was the average cost per month?

_____ 6. In the years 1994 to 1996, space shuttle *Atlantis* flew 10 missions, space shuttle *Discovery* flew 8 missions, and space shuttle *Columbia* flew 12 missions. If each flight cost $300,000,000, how much was spent during those 3 years?

_____ 7. About 400,000 people watched the *Discovery*'s safe return to Earth. There was a 5-man crew. How many spectators were there for each crew member?

_____ 8. One space mission for *Discovery* lasted 4 days, 1 hour, and 57 seconds. To the nearest minute, how many minutes did it last?

_____ 9. An estimated 109,000 vehicles carried about 400,000 spectators to watch the *Discovery* land. What was the average number of people in each vehicle? (Round to the nearest hundredth.)

_____ 10. A vendor at the site of the space landing was selling flags for $2.00. If 1/10 of the 400,000 people watching bought a flag, what was the total sales amount?

Space Figures

_____ 11. When a shuttle enters Earth's atmosphere for a landing, it is traveling at 25 times the speed of sound. If the speed of sound is 750 miles an hour, how fast is the shuttle going?

_____ 12. A space shuttle orbits Earth 184 miles high. A mile is 5,280 feet. How many feet is the space shuttle above Earth?

_____ 13. Boosters for a space shuttle are 149 feet long. They weigh 200,000 pounds. What is the weight per foot? (Round to the nearest hundredth.)

_____ 14. If the space shuttle _Atlantis_ is launched at 9:31 a.m. (EST) on September 25 for a mission to dock with the _Mir_ space station, and the expected flight duration is 10 days, 3 hours, and 49 minutes, at what date and time (EST) will _Atlantis_ land?

_____ 15. The overall length of the space shuttle is about 184 feet. The overall weight is 4,521,762 pounds. What is the average weight per foot?

_____ 16. The space shuttle _Orbiter_ is 122 feet long. The weight is 165,000 pounds. What is the weight per foot? (Round to the nearest hundredth.)

_____ 17. _Discovery's_ basic mission was to launch a $100,000,000 tracking satellite. The satellite weighed 4,900 pounds. How much did it cost per pound? (Round to the nearest hundredth.)

_____ 18. Improved life-support systems in the space shuttles make 18-day flights possible. How many minutes is that?

_____ 19. Two solid rocket boosters and three main engines on the _Orbiter_ are needed for liftoff thrust to put the space shuttle in space. It takes 6,500,000 pounds of thrust for launching. If each solid rocket booster provides 2,658,000 pounds of thrust, how many pounds do the three _Orbiter_ engines provide?

_____ 20. The cost of sending the shuttle _Discovery_ into space was $300,000,000. The shuttle covered 1,680,000 miles. What was the cost per mile to the nearest hundredth?

Go Figure!

1. When you are resting, your heart pumps about 3 quarts of blood each minute, and when you are running or working hard, it pumps 24 quarts. If you work 8 hours and rest the other part of the day, how many quarts of blood will your heart pump in one day? one week? one month (30 days)? one year? Show your calculations on the back of this sheet.

   _____ 1 day   _____ 1 week

   _____ 1 month   _____ 1 year

2. Each time your heart beats it moves 3 ounces of blood, approximately 10 tons each day. Solve these mathematical problems to get a better understanding of how hard your heart works for you. How many pounds of blood does your heart pump in one day? one week? one month? one year? Show your calculations on the back of this paper.

   _____ 1 day   _____ 1 week

   _____ 1 month   _____ 1 year

3. If joined end to end, your blood vessels would be 60,000 miles long. It is difficult to imagine how long that is. Use an encyclopedia to find out the approximate circumference of Earth and the moon in miles. Then calculate approximately how many times the vessels in your body would wrap around Earth and the moon. Show your calculations on the back of this paper.

   _____ Earth   _____ moon

   _____ circumference

4. If joined side by side, the blood vessels in your body would make a pipe 800 inches in diameter. Approximately how many feet is that? how many yards?

   _____ feet   _____ yards

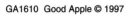

Dinosaur Math

Most dinosaurs were huge, fierce-looking animals, but some were no larger than a very small dog. Dinosaurs lived on land. There were other huge animals during the dinosaur age that could fly, and many others lived in the water. The object of this quiz is to figure out these giants of Earth.

_____ 1. The dinosaur Antarctosaurus weighed about 80 tons. How many pounds did it weigh?

_____ 2. Brachiosaurus was about 40 feet tall. A giraffe is about 18 feet tall. Brachiosaurus was how many times taller than the giraffe?

_____ 3. A thoroughbred horse can run 1 1/4 miles in 2 minutes. The dinosaur Gallinimus could run 35 miles an hour. In a race between a thoroughbred and Gallinimus, which would be the winner?

4. Some of the faster dinosaurs could walk about 12 miles per hour. Some human beings can run a mile in 15 minutes.

_____ a. How many minutes would it take a dinosaur to walk a mile?

_____ b. How many miles could a human run in an hour?

_____ 5. Tyrannosaurus Rex was about 15 meters long. How many feet is that?

_____ 6. Laid end to end, how many 6-feet-3-inch-tall humans would it take to equal the length of Tyrannosaurus Rex?

_____ 7. The first dinosaurs were only 3 feet long. Millions of years later, Apatosaurus was about 80 feet long. How many times longer was Apatosaurus than its ancestor?

_____ 8. Dinosaurs first appeared about 210 million years ago and suddenly disappeared about 65 million years ago. How long was the dinosaur age?

GA1610 Good Apple © 1997

Dinosaur Math

_____ 9. The average human life span is about 73 years. Large dinosaurs lived about 100 years. On the average, how many more days did a dinosaur live than a human?

_____10. Kareem Abdul Jabbar, the great basketball player, is 7 feet, 2 inches tall. Approximately how many Jabbars would it take to equal the length of Triceratops, who was 30 feet long?

_____11. Tyrannosaurus Rex, a dinosaur that ate other dinosaurs, had a large mouth filled with 6-inch teeth. The largest human tooth (canine) is about 3/8 of an inch long. How many human teeth would it take to make 1 Tyrannosaurus tooth?

_____12. The Anatosaurus had 2,000 teeth. A human has 32. How many sets of human teeth would it take to make 1 set for Anatosaurus?

_____13. The eggs of huge dinosaurs were small. A dinosaur 40 feet long might lay an egg only 12 inches long. What was the percentage of the egg's length to the dinosaur that laid it?

_____14. The cave spider lays an egg 1/4 the size of its body. If a 40-foot dinosaur laid an egg 1/4 the size of its body, how long would the egg have been?

_____15. Ankylosaurus was about 35 feet tall. An African male elephant is 11 1/2 feet tall. Approximately how many times taller was Ankylosaurus than the elephant?

_____16. As large as the dinosaurs were, the blue whale that lives today is probably larger with a length of 95 feet and weight of 150 tons. Brachiosaurus was about 40 feet long and weighed about 80 tons. How many more pounds does the blue whale weigh than Brachiosaurus?

Graph It!

Animals have different heartbeat rates. The hummingbird has a heartbeat rate of 800 to 1,000 beats per minute. Use the chart of heartbeat rates below to design your graph. Choose eight animals and graph the highest rate shown for each. Calculate your heartbeat rate and include yourself on your graph.

canary	500 to 800	mouse	350 to 800	cat	120 to 140
pig	70 to 80	chicken	300 to 350	rabbit	140 to 160
dog	70 to 120	rat	260 to 600	elephant	25 to 50
sheep	70 to 80	horse	30 to 50	lion	40 to 50
hummingbird	800 to 1,000				

GA1610 Good Apple © 1997

Cleaning Up Our Home

Each of the two blocks below is divided into 20 boxes. Boxes in the top block contain problems and boxes in the bottom block contain the answers. Work the problems and find the answers in the bottom block. Then write the words from the problem boxes into the correct answer boxes to find a message about our Earth.

84 x 38 Earth	255 x 43 It's	408 x 53 everything	27 x 73 the	75 x 66 home
895 x 68 to	64 x 29 only	72 x 76 Spaceship	706 x 24 it	273 x 96 do
93 x 66 is	47 x 34 have	805 x 73 protect	623 x 79 on	907 x 27 we
367 x 56 counting	604 x 89 to	784 x 38 us	93 x 88 we	305 x 46 can

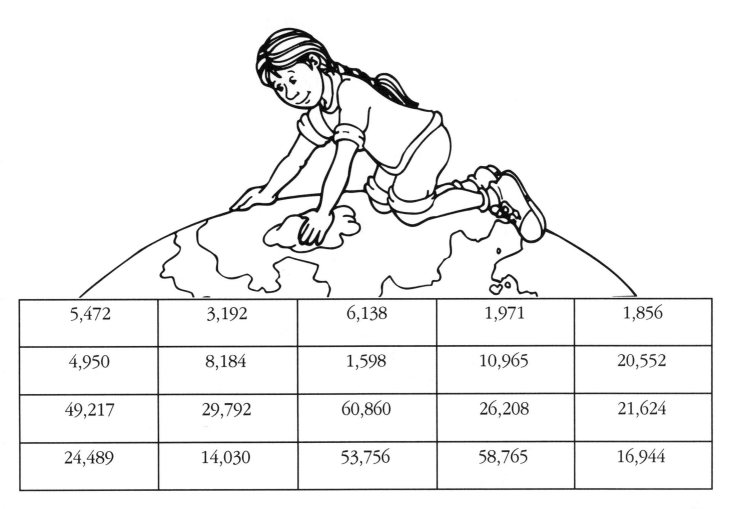

5,472	3,192	6,138	1,971	1,856
4,950	8,184	1,598	10,965	20,552
49,217	29,792	60,860	26,208	21,624
24,489	14,030	53,756	58,765	16,944

Math History

_____ 1. What is the total when you add the year Paul Revere took his famous ride and the number of original colonies?

_____ 2. Add the year the Declaration of Independence was signed and the year the United States Constitution was written.

_____ 3. What is the total when you add bicentennial, sesquicentennial and centennial?

_____ 4. Add the number of U.S. representatives, the number of U.S. senators, and the number of Supreme Court justices.

_____ 5. Add the years Jamestown, Virginia, and Plymouth, Massachusetts, were settled.

_____ 6. Subtract the number of stripes in the United States flag from the number of stars.

_____ 7. Subtract the year the Declaration of Independence was signed from the year the Civil War began.

_____ 8. Subtract the number of presidents who have been shot from the total number of presidents.

_____ 9. Subtract the number of wars the United States fought in the nineteenth century from the number they fought in the twentieth century.

_____ 10. What is the difference between the number of actual signers of the United States Constitution and the number of presidents?

GA1610 Good Apple © 1997

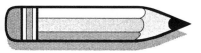

Math History

_____ 11. Multiply the 22nd Amendment times the number of years it allows a president to serve.

_____ 12. Multiply the number of senators allowed each state by the number of states.

_____ 13. Multiply the number of presidents named Adams by the number named Harrison and divide the sum by the number named Roosevelt.

_____ 14. Give the fraction of votes needed in the United States Senate to impeach a president.

_____ 15. Divide the age of the nation in 1997 by the number of United States presidents (to 1997) to find the average number of years served by all presidents.

_____ 16. Eight presidents were born in Virginia. What percent of presidents have come from Virginia?

_____ 17. Both the president of the Union and the president of the Confederacy (Abraham Lincoln and Jefferson Davis, respectively) were born in Kentucky. What percent of United States presidents was born in Kentucky?

_____ What percent of Confederate presidents was born in Kentucky?

_____ 18. Thirty-five and seven-tenths percent of the presidents were born in Ohio and Virginia. What is the total number of presidents from these two states?

_____ 19. Both John Adams and Thomas Jefferson died July 4, 1826. If Adams was 91, in what year was he born? If Jefferson was 83, in what year was he born?

Edison Math

Thomas Edison did not like mathematics but math was necessary for his complicated inventions. Demonstrate that you could have helped Mr. Edison by finding the correct solutions to these problems.

_____ 1. Edison sold an improvement of the stock ticker to Gold and Stock Telegraph Company for $40,000. He was 23 at the time. How much did that average for each year of his life?

_____ 2. Edison was offered $100,000 for his improvement of the telephone. He chose to receive payments of $6,000 a year. For how many years did he receive the money?

_____ 3. If he had taken the $100,000 and invested it at 4% interest, how much more would he have made in the same number of years?

_____ 4. If a light bulb costs 69 cents and lasts 300 hours, what is the cost per hour?

_____ 5. Edison had 2,000 employees. If they were paid an average wage of 40 cents an hour, what was the
a. weekly payroll (5 days, 8 hours per day) ?   b. yearly payroll (50 weeks)?

_____ 6. Edison had 1,100 patents. What is 6/10 of 1,100?

_____ 7. If Edison contracted to lay 20 miles of electric wire and a crew could lay 1,000 feet a day, how many days would it take him?

_____ 8. Edison lost $3,000,000 mining for iron ore in New Jersey and another $5,000,000 when his laboratories burned in West Orange, New Jersey. He lived to be 84. What were his average losses per year?

_____ 9. Suppose Edison made $17,000,000 in his lifetime. What were his average earnings per year?

_____ 10. Subtract his losses (Question 8) from his estimated earnings (Question 9). What were his average net earnings?

_____ 11. Thomas Edison had 6 children; 2 were girls. What percentage of his children were girls?

_____ 12. Thomas Edison was married from 1871 until 1884 and 1886 to 1931. What were his total married years?

_____ 13. Edison's father died in 1896 at the age of 92. Edison was born in 1847. How old was the father when Thomas Edison was born?

_____ 14. Using the answer from Question 12, calculate what percentage of Edison's life was spent in marriage.

_____ 15. In 1929, the golden anniversary of the electric light was celebrated.
a. How many years is that?   b. How old was Edison at the time?

GA1610 Good Apple © 1997

Martin Luther King, Jr.'s Life
in Numbers

26 1965 73

56

73 20,000

Martin
Luther King,
Jr.

1957

_____ 1. Martin Luther King, Jr., was killed when he was 39. The average life span in the United States is about 73. What percentage of the average life span (to the nearest percent) did King live?

_____ 2. John F. Kennedy was 46 years old when he was assassinated, and Abraham Lincoln was 56. What was the combined ages of Lincoln, King, and Kennedy?

_____ 3. In the Montgomery, Alabama, bus boycott of 1955 and 1956, 17,000 blacks refused to ride buses for 382 days. What was the total number of bus fares lost to the boycott?

_____ 4. At a fare of 20 cents per ride, what was the total amount of money lost on fares by the bus company?

_____ 5. In the Little Rock, Arkansas, crisis of 1957, 11,000 National Guardsmen were present to make certain nine black students entered Little Rock High School. What was the ratio of National Guardsmen to black students?

_____ 6. 200,000 people attended the March on Washington protest demonstration. If each person walked an average of 50 miles, how many total miles did the people walk?

_____ 7. Approximately how many times would that be to the moon (240,000 miles)?

_____ 8. The march from Selma, Alabama, to the state capital in Montgomery was 54 miles. 25,000 marchers took part. What were the total miles covered by all marchers?

_____ 9. On May 26, 1965, the United States Senate passed the voting rights bill by a vote margin of 77 to 19. What percentage of senators voted no?

_____ 10. In 1964, Martin Luther King, Jr., was awarded the Nobel Peace Prize. He received $54,000. He was 35 at the time. How much money was that for each year of his life?

Important Dates in
Marie Curie's Life

Marie was one of the top students in mathematics at the university she attended. How well do you know your math? Complete the problems below and write the answers on the lines. The answers will be important dates pertaining to the life of Marie Curie. Write the letter of the problem next to the matching date in the puzzle blanks. The letters will spell a mystery word.

N   Marie's second daughter was born in
(1330 – 854) x (52 ÷ 13)   _____

I   Marie graduated with honors from the Gymnasium in
(36 x 33) + (139 x 5)   _____

L   Marie and Pierre announced the existence of polonium and radium in
(667 + 282) x (648 ÷ 324)   _____

P   Marya Sklodowska (later known as Marie Curie) was born in
(52 x 13) + (7146 ÷ 6)   _____

D   Marie won the Nobel Prize in chemistry in
(2051 – 689) + (183 x 3)   _____

E   Marie and Pierre Curie received the Nobel Prize in physics in
(14,863 + 9876) ÷ (208 ÷ 16)   _____

H   Marie married Pierre Curie in
(1137 x 5) ÷ (87 ÷ 29)   _____

T   Marie began courses at the Sorbonne in
(9000 – 1436) ÷ (516 ÷ 129)   _____

B   Marie and Pierre's first daughter, Irène, was born in
(2631 – 99) – (127 x 5)   _____

C   Marie finished first in physics in her class in
(62 x 37) – (237 + 164)   _____

E   Marie died in
(3908 + 2634) – (144 x 32)   _____

____ ____ ____ ____ ____ ____ ____ ____ ____ ____ ____
1867 1883 1891 1893 1895 1897 1898 1903 1904 1911 1934

Tell about the mystery word's significance to Marie Curie's research. _____

_____

_____

_____

GA1610 Good Apple © 1997

The Wright Brothers

Wilbur Wright was born on April 16, 1867, on a farm in Indiana. Orville Wright was born on August 19, 1871, in Dayton, Ohio. Both of the brothers had inventive minds, were good readers, and had a gift for craftsmanship.

The two boys were greatly impressed with a toy helicopter their father brought home. It was constructed of cork, bamboo, and thin paper and was driven by twisted rubber bands. Wilbur tried to build bigger helicopters when he was 11. He soon discovered that the bigger they were, the more difficult they were to fly. Orville started building kites a few years later. He soon learned that for a kite to fly well, it must be as light as possible. The Wright Brothers never lost their desire to explore flying.

Wilbur and Orville were both athletic and became enthusiastic cyclists. In 1895, they began to repair and manufacture bicycles. Fortunately, the bicycle business was seasonal, and the brothers were only busy in the spring and early summer. In autumn, they were free to make and test flying machines.

On December 14, 1903, they tossed a coin to see which of them would have the privilege of being the first to make a motorized flight. Wilbur won the toss and successfully flew the first airplane powered by a gasoline engine at Kitty Hawk at a speed of about 30 miles per hour.

On September 9, 1908, Orville made 57 complete circles at an altitude of 120 feet at Fort Myer, Virginia. This flight lasted one hour and two minutes and set several records. Both men continued building and flying airplanes until they died. Wilbur Wright lived until 1912, and his brother, Orville, lived until 1948.

Use the facts found in the story to solve these arithmetic problems.

1. How old was Wilbur when Orville was born? _____

2. In what year did Wilbur try to build a bigger toy helicopter? _____

3. How old were the brothers at the turn of the century? _____

4. How old was each boy when they began repairing and manufacturing bicycles? _____

5. How old was Wilbur when he successfully flew the first gasoline-engine-powered airplane at Kitty Hawk? _____

6. How old was Orville when he set flight records at Fort Myer, Virginia? _____

7. How old was Orville when his brother, Wilbur, died? _____

8. In what year was Wilbur exactly three times his brother's age? _____

9. In what year was Orville exactly half his brother's age? _____

10. How old was each brother when he died? _____

Grandma Moses' Math

In the South (1887-1905), both Grandma Moses and her husband worked hard to earn a living. In order to farm, they bought a span of horses, cows, hens, and implements. Following are prices paid for three items:

1 cow	$25.00
1 cow	$27.00
12 hens	$ 6.00 (from which 18 chicks hatched)

1. What was the total amount spent?_____

2. What was the average price per cow? _____

3. What was the price per hen? _____

4. If we assume that each chick became fully grown, how much did each fowl actually cost? _____

5. Besides purchase price, what other expenses would there be for keeping:

   a) cows? _____, _____

   b) chickens? _____, _____

6. We have no record of egg sales. However, dairy products were itemized. Grandma Moses washed and filled 60 to 100 bottles of milk daily. There were 20 bottles in a box.
   How many boxes did it take daily for 60 bottles? _____ for 100 bottles? _____

7. How many bottles were sold weekly at 60 bottles per day? _____
   How many boxes were used? _____

8. How many bottles were sold weekly at 100 bottles per day? _____
   How many boxes were used? _____

9. Although prices paid for milk were not recorded, butter prices were given. At first, Grandma Moses received only $0.15 per pound, then $0.20, and finally $0.50 per pound. She made 20 prints (pounds) to a tray; 4 trays to a crate. She sold 2 crates per week.
   How many pounds would there be in a crate? _____

10. How many pounds did she sell per week?_____

Grandma Moses' Math

11. At $0.15 per pound, how much did she take in weekly? _____ At $0.20? _____
    At $0.50? _____

12. For homemade potato chips, Grandma received in trade at the grocery store $0.25 for a one-pound bag, then $0.30 for a one-pound bag.
    How much did she take in for 5 pounds at $0.25 per bag? _____ 10 pounds? _____

13. How much did she take in for 5 pounds at $0.30 per bag? _____ 10 pounds? _____

14. Following is Grandma Moses' recipe for making apple butter in quantity:
    2 barrels of sweet cider   Cook over an outdoor fire. Stir continuously.
    3 barrels of apples, quartered   (Young people took turns stirring from morning
    20 (or more) pounds of sugar   to midnight.) Store in 1-gallon stone jugs. (She
    cinnamon or clove oil to taste   usually filled 40 jars.)
    What was the total number of barrels of apples plus cider?

15. Since about 40 gallons of apple butter were produced, how many gallons were made per barrel?
    _____

16. Making apple butter was a social occasion. Explain. _____
    _____

17. A load of fresh vegetables went into town every other day for 6 months (about April through September).
    About how many total trips were made (using 30 days per month)? _____

18. Name two travel expenses they would have had. _____ _____

19. What vegetables might have been grown in Virginia? _____, _____,
    _____, _____

Presidential Mathematics

You will need a chart showing dates of birth, death, and term of office for the U.S. presidents to complete this exercise. Check the encyclopedia or almanac.

_____ 1. Who lived longer, Chester A. Arthur or Franklin Pierce?

_____ 2. In 1997, how many total years had the United States had a president?

_____ 3. If the average number of children per president is 3, about how many presidential children have there been in all?

_____ 4. What fraction of the presidents has a first name beginning with "J"?

_____ 5. What is the average number of years the first 5 presidents lived?

_____ 6. What percentage of presidents were born in the 18th century?

_____ 7. Divide the total number of presidents by the number with first names beginning with "W."

_____ 8. How old was Martin Van Buren when William H. Taft was born?

Inauguration Ages

Listed below are the presidents of the United States and their ages at the time of their inaugurations. Their ages are given to you in Roman numerals. Figure out each age and then answer the questions.

1. George Washington LVII = _____
2. John Adams LXI = _____
3. Thomas Jefferson LVII = _____
4. James Madison LVII = _____
5. James Monroe LVIII = _____
6. John Quincy Adams LVII = _____
7. Andrew Jackson LXI = _____
8. Martin Van Buren LIV = _____
9. William Henry Harrison LXVIII = _____
10. John Tyler LI = _____
11. James K. Polk XLIX = _____
12. Zachary Taylor LXIV = _____
13. Millard Fillmore L = _____
14. Franklin Pierce XLVIII = _____
15. James Buchanan LXV = _____
16. Abraham Lincoln LII = _____
17. Andrew Johnson LVI = _____
18. Ulysses S. Grant XLVI = _____
19. Rutherford B. Hayes LIV = _____
20. James Garfield XLIX = _____
21. Chester A. Arthur LI = _____

22. Grover Cleveland XLVII = _____
23. Benjamin Harrison LV = _____
24. William McKinley LIV = _____
25. Theodore Roosevelt XLII = _____
26. William H. Taft LI = _____
27. Woodrow Wilson LVI = _____
28. Warren G. Harding LV = _____
29. Calvin Coolidge LI = _____
30. Herbert Hoover LIV = _____
31. Franklin D. Roosevelt LI = _____
32. Harry S. Truman LX = _____
33. Dwight D. Eisenhower LXII = _____
34. John F. Kennedy XLIII = _____
35. Lyndon B. Johnson LV = _____
36. Richard M. Nixon LVI = _____
37. Gerald Ford LXI = _____
38. Jimmy Carter LII = _____
39. Ronald Reagan LXIX = _____
40. George Bush LXIV = _____
41. Bill Clinton XLVI = _____

1. Who was the youngest man ever to be inaugurated president? _____

2. How many men were 58 years old when inaugurated? _____

3. Who was the oldest man ever inaugurated? _____

4. Of the last 10 presidents, who was the youngest? _____
   the oldest? _____

5. How much older was Ronald Reagan than Abraham Lincoln when inaugurated? _____

McGuffey's Math

_____ 1. From 1836 to 1920, McGuffey's Reader sold 122,000,000 copies. What was the average number of Readers sold each year (to the nearest whole number)?

_____ 2. If McGuffey's Reader sold for 75¢ per copy, what was the total amount that all the Readers in Question #1 sold for?

_____ 3. If William McGuffey received 10% of the total amount, how much money did he receive for his Readers?

_____ 4. William McGuffey was born in 1800 and died in 1873. About how many months did he live?

_____ 5. McGuffey graduated from Washington College in 1829. He died in 1873. How many years did he live after he graduated from college?

_____ 6. When McGuffey attended Greersburg Academy, he paid 75¢ a week for meals. If he attended the Academy year-round for 2 years, how much did he pay for meals?

_____ 7. By 1836, the combined population of Ohio, Kentucky, Tennessee, Indiana, Michigan, and Illinois was over 9,000,000. About 1,800,000 of this population was of school age. What percent of the total population was of school age?

_____ 8. In 1836, Ohio had a population of 1,000,000. 461,000 were immigrants. What percent of the total population was made up of immigrants?

_____ 9. There were 153 pictures in McGuffey's First Reader. 102 were of animal life. What percent of the pictures were of other subjects?

GA1610 Good Apple © 1997

McGuffey's Math

_____ 10. In the Second Reader of 1838 there were 33 lessons about boys and only 7 about girls. About how many more times were stories about boys than girls?

_____ 11. McGuffey's favorite animal was the dog. 200 dog stories appeared in his first through sixth Readers. What was the average number of dog stories per Reader? (Round to the nearest whole number.)

_____ 12. McGuffey lived to be 73 and taught 38 years. What percent of his life was not involved in teaching? (Round to the nearest hundredth.)

_____ 13. William McGuffey taught 6 years in elementary schools. Of his 38 years of teaching, what percent was spent at the college level?

_____ 14. William McGuffey was the second child in a family of 11 children. Counting his mother and father, what percent of the family did William comprise? (Round to the nearest hundredth.)

_____ 15. William McGuffey had 6 children. Four died before the age of 17. What percent of his children reached adulthood?

_____ 16. McGuffey was born in 1800. If he had lived, how many candles would he have on his birthday cake on September 23, 1994?

_____ 17. McGuffey was born 9 years before Abraham Lincoln and lived 8 years after Lincoln's death. Lincoln was 56 when he was assassinated. How old was McGuffey when he died?

18. Alexander McGuffey, William's youngest brother, was born in 1816. He was the author of McGuffey's Fifth Reader, published in 1844.

_____ a. How old was Alexander when the book was issued?

_____ b. How old was William McGuffey (born in 1800)?

Civil War Numbers

The Civil War (1861-1865) was fought between the North (Union) and the South (Confederacy) to preserve our union and free the slaves. The number of soldiers involved and the loss of lives was awesome. The loss of soldiers (the actual loss of civilian lives is unknown) in the Civil War is equal to the lives lost in all other wars in which this country has fought.

_____ 1. In the presidential election of 1860, Abraham Lincoln received 180 electoral votes. His three opponents received 123. What percentage of electoral votes did Lincoln get?

_____ 2. Abraham Lincoln was born February 12, 1809, and died from a bullet at the hands of John Wilkes Booth on April 15, 1865. What were the exact number of years and days of his life?

_____ 3. In the election of 1864, Abraham Lincoln received 212 electoral votes and George B. McClellan received 21. What percentage of electoral votes did Lincoln get? (Round to the nearest tenth.)

_____ 4. Lincoln received 2,206,938 popular votes; McClellan 1,803,787. How many more popular votes did Lincoln receive?

_____ 5. In 1861, the population of the United States was 32,351,000. The South had a population of 9,000,000. What percentage of the total population did the North have?

_____ 6. Jefferson Davis, president of the Confederacy, was born June 3, 1808, and died December 6, 1881. How many more years and days did he live than Lincoln?

_____ 7. The Civil War started April 12, 1861, and ended April 9, 1865. How many years and days did the war last?

_____ 8. Before the Civil War ended, the North had an army of approximately 1,000,000. Of that number 360,000 lost their lives What percentage of soldiers lost their lives?

_____ 9. In 1860, there were 4,000,000 slaves in the South and 250,000 free blacks. What percentage of the blacks were free? (Round to the nearest tenth.)

_____ 10. 200,000 blacks fought for the North. What percentage of the Union army was black?

GA1610 Good Apple © 1997

Civil War Numbers

_____ 11. 260,000 Confederate soldiers lost their lives in the Civil War. What was the total loss of lives for the North and South in the Civil War?

_____ 12. In the important battle of Gettysburg, July 1–3, 1863, the North had an army of 90,000; the South had 75,000. What was the number of men who fought the battle?

_____ 13. The North suffered 18,000 casualties at Gettysburg. What was their percentage of army casualties?

_____ 14. The South had 20,000 casualties at Gettysburg. What was their percentage of casualties? (Round to the nearest tenth.)

_____ 15. General Ulysses S. Grant was 63 when he died. He spent 4 years in the Union army. What percentage of his life did he spend in the Union army?

_____ 16. Grant was president for 8 years. What percentage of his life was spent as president? (Round to the nearest percent.)

_____ 17. General Robert E. Lee, the Confederate general, was born in 1807 and died in 1870. How did the length of his life compare to Grant's?

_____ 18. What was the combined number of years that Lee, Grant, and Lincoln lived? What was their average age? (Round to the nearest tenth.)

_____ 19. General Lee was a soldier for 40 years. What percentage of his life was spent as a soldier? (Round to the nearest percent.)

_____ 20. In 1861, the population of the United States was 32,351,000. In 1988, the population of the country was about 240,000,000. Approximately how many times has the population increased in 127 years? (Round to the nearest hundredth.)

Trail Math

_____ 1. The United States bought 827,987 square miles from France for $15,000,000 in what was known as the Louisiana Purchase. What was the cost per square mile to the nearest cent?

_____ 2. If there are 640 acres in a square mile, how many acres were purchased?

_____ 3. To the nearest cent, what was the cost per acre?

_____ 4. Assuming a journey from New York to Los Angeles is 3,000 miles and an oxen caravan covered 12 miles per day, how many days did it take to reach the destination?

5. It takes an Amtrak train 2 days and 14 hours to cover the same distance.
_____ a. How many miles per hour is the train traveling?
_____ b. A plane makes the trip in 6 hours. How many miles per hour is the plane traveling?

_____ 6. In 1848, when the Mormons started their trek to Salt Lake City, they took 923 wagons and 4,000 oxen. What was the average number of oxen per wagon?

_____ 7. 2,400 people were on the trek. What was the average number of people per wagon?

8. The discovery of gold in California greatly increased the migration to the West. In a 3-year period, the value of the gold found in California was $41,000,000; $75,000,000; and $81,000,000.
_____ a. What was the total for the 3 years?
_____ b. What was the average?

_____ 9. One rider for the Pony Express could cover 160 miles in 9 hours. How many miles could he cover in 1 hour?

_____ 10. When the Con Virginia silver mine's worth was estimated, one group said $230,000,000; another man said $1,500,000,000. What was the difference in the estimates?

84

Trail Math

_____ 11. When the Con Virginia stock was placed on the stock market, it went from $90 to $790 a share. How many times did it increase?

_____ 12. On the Lewis and Clark expedition, hunters bagged 131 elk between December 1, 1805, and March 20, 1806. How many elk did the hunters average per day?

_____ 13. In one 24-hour period, a man observed 900 wagons pass along the Oregon Trail. How many wagons was that per hour?

14. In 1841, 20 wagons and 69 pioneers traveled the Oregon Trail. In 1850, Army officers counted 44,527 people and 9,927 wagons.
_____ a. How many times more people passed in 1850 than in 1841?
_____ b. How many times more wagons passed in 1850 than in 1841?

15. What was the average number of people and wagons per day in 1850 to the nearest whole number?
_____ a. Average number of people?
_____ b. Average number of wagons?

_____ 16. In the early West, one sheep rancher purchased 9,000 sheep for $5,000. How much did he pay per head, to the nearest cent?

_____ 17. The next year he sold his flock, now grown to 18,000 sheep for 75¢ a head. How much profit did he make?

_____ 18. Kit Carson bought 6,500 sheep for $2.50 a head. He took them to California and sold them for $30,000 profit. How much did he sell them for?

_____ 19. A cattle rancher bought 10,000 longhorns for $1 a head. He took them on a cattle drive to Dodge City, Kansas, losing 800 along the way, and sold them for $5 a head. His total expenses for hired help were $2,000. How much profit did he make?

_____ 20. Thomas Jefferson authorized the price of $9,375,000 for the Floridas and New Orleans. Instead, James Monroe, later to be president, paid $15,000,000 for the much larger Louisiana Purchase. How much more was paid than Jefferson authorized?

A Romp With Roman Numerals

Roman numerals are written with seven basic symbols: I (1), V (5), X (10), L (50), C (100), D (500) and M (1,000). All other numbers are a combination of these seven symbols. Except for numbers beginning with 4 or 9, Roman numerals use the principle of addition. For example, 25 is written XXV (10 + 10 + 5). The numbers 4 and 9, and any numbers beginning with 4 or 9, use the principle of subtraction. For example, 4 is written IV (5 - 1) and 90 is written XC (100 - 10). To solve the arithmetic problems below, first convert the Roman numerals into Arabic numbers. Can you write the answers in Roman numerals?

1. VIII = _____
    x V = x_____
    ____ = _____

2. XXXIII = _____
    + XVII = +_____
    _____ = _____

3. LXIX = _____
    – XI = –_____
    ____ = _____

4. C = _____
    CX = _____
    + CXL = +_____
    _____ = _____

5. MMM = _____
    – MDCC = –_____
    _____ = _____

6. CMXCIX = _____
    ÷ III = ÷_____
    ____ = _____

7. DCCXVIII = _____
    –CLXXXVII = –_____
    _____ = _____

8. DLXXV = _____
    + MMDCXLIV = +_____
    _____ = _____

To write numbers larger than 3,999 a bar is placed over a number to show that it is multiplied by 1,000. For example, 5,000 is written $\overline{V}$ (5 x 1000) and 4,000 is written $M\overline{V}$ (5000 - 1000). How would you write the following numbers in Roman numerals?

1. 10,000 _____

2. 25,000 _____

3. 50,000 _____

4. 100,000 _____

5. 1,000,000 _____

6. 5,000,000 _____

7. 10,000,000 _____

8. 13,524 _____

Can you write the following number in Arabic numerals?
MMMMMMMMMMDCCCLXXXIV   ____ ____, ____ ____ ____

Can you name three places the Roman numeral system is used today?
1. _____
2. _____
3. _____

GA1610 Good Apple © 1997

Mythology Design
Apollo, God of the Sun

Work the problem in each square. Look at your answer. Use the color key under the Apollo grid to tell you what color to make that square or part of the square. Do each square in the same way. You will create the design for Apollo, God of the Sun.

 0-10, yellow   11-20, yellow   21-30, yellow   31-40, yellow   41-50, yellow

51-60, orange   61-70, orange   71-80, orange   81-90, orange   91-100, orange

					100 − 32	16 ×6						
				85 − 17	35 + 19	5/300	10 ×10					
	121 − 68	4/204	18 ×3	162 − 73				42 + 37	5/300	81 − 22	13 ×4	
	12 ×5	106 − 51	14 ×6		455 − 439	6 2 +1	16/96	11 ×4		362 − 288	13 12 +35	8/408
	10 ×6	105 − 16		12 + 7	125 ×0	172 − 163	89/445	2 2 +6	7 ×7		20 14 +42	4/240
	21 ×4		92 − 73	163 − 159	21 21 +21	6/36	1/10	30 20 +20	72/360	(5x5) x 2		731 − 652
42 11 +15		15/285	541 ×0	361 − 360	10/90	5 1 +2	1/4	5/45	32 − 28	0 +0	12 ×4		31 31 +31
5/365		71 − 42	777 ×0	1 2 +3	19 − 17	8 ×4 / 13 ×5	20 +2 / 100 −8	9/81	25 − 25	35/35	10 11 +12		11 ×8
	2/200		7 ×3	24/120	96 ×0	845 − 842	(1x2) +6	60/180	3 2 +2	702 − 671		(9x4)+33
	32 12 +16	33 ×3		(5x2)+20	10 ×5 / 9 ×8	19 11 +25	731 − 680	11 ×8 / 13 ×1	19 ×2		16 ×4	701 − 650
	18 18 +18	3/156	11 ×9		13 ×2	745 ×0	19/95	344 − 312		36 + 25	11 ×5	20 20 +20
	19 ×3	500 − 449	17 + 36	(7x7)+50				12/840	(8x3)+32	771 − 711	7 ×8
					13 ×6	18 19 +20	10/600	22 ×4				
					747 − 668	(9x6)+30						

Mayan Numbers

The ancient Maya developed a numbering system which was based on 20 digits, from 0 to 19. Zero was signified by the "shell," which also symbolized the concept of completion. Other numerals were represented by a combination of dots and lines. Each dot was a unit and each line signified "a handful" of units, or 5. Beyond 19, dots and lines were still used, but in a place value system, which allowed large numbers, common in their advanced computations and calendars, to be easily written. Look at the numbers below, then complete the math problems using Mayan digits.

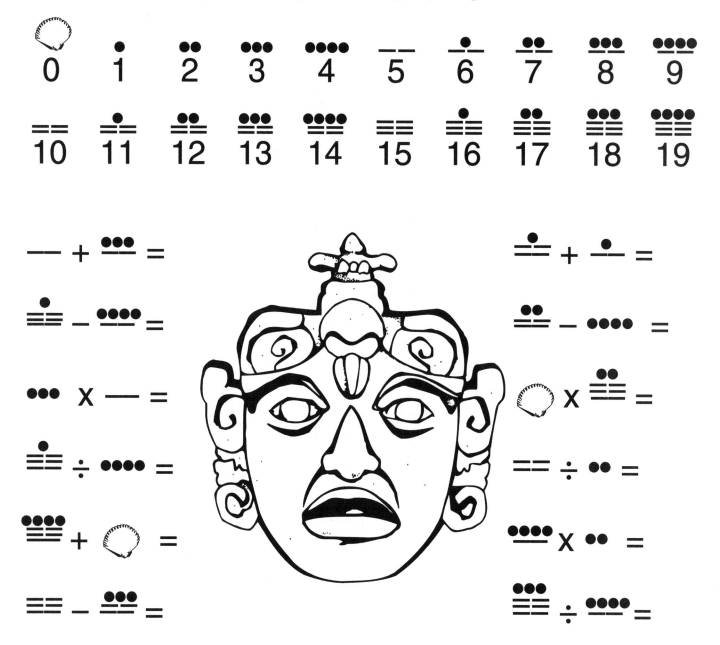

Car Computing

_____ 1. The list price on a pickup truck is $7,874. There is a clearance discount of $879 and a rebate of $300. What is the purchase price of the pickup?

_____ 2. The interest charge on the pickup truck described above is 3.7%. How much interest will the buyer pay the first year?

_____ 3. A pickup truck can be purchased for $7,547. An advertisement states it can be paid for at only $31.32 per week. How many weeks will it take to pay for the pickup? How many months?

_____ 4. A car that costs $12,749 in 1983 can be purchased for $6,210 four years later. What was the average depreciation per year?

_____ 5. Car A sells for $13,990 but the buyer will receive a 10% rebate. Car B sells for $13,990 with no rebate, but there is no charge for air conditioning ($825) and automatic transmission ($560) (which are on both cars). Which car is the better deal?

_____ 6. A new pickup truck sells for $7,890. Dealer A offers an interest rate of 3.7% for 2 years. Dealer B offers 3.9% for 2 years. What is the difference in the amount paid to Dealer A and that paid to Dealer B?

_____ 7. A car is advertised at $7090 with a $750 rebate and a 3.9% interest rate for 2 years. What will be the total cost of the car?

_____ 8. A car sells for $7,495. There is a choice of a rebate of $1,500 and a 6.9% interest charge for 3 years or no rebate and 3.7% interest charged for 3 years. Which is the better deal?

_____ 9. There are two identical cars for sale. One is priced for $11,200, which includes transportation charges. The other is $10,980, but the buyer must pay the transportation charges (transportation charges are $450). Which is cheaper?

_____ 10. If the list price of a car is $13,995 but there is a rebate of $600, finance savings of $770, and an equipment discount of $800, what is the percent of savings? (Round to the nearest tenth.)

continued

Car Computing

_____ 11. A car priced at $15,402 was not sold. When the new models came out, the car was offered for $12,796. What was the percent of reduction?

_____ 12. A car dealer offers a cash rebate of $1,000, an equipment discount of $400, and a cellular mobile telephone that lists for $1,400 for $395. If a buyer purchases the car for $13,990, what is the full list price?

_____ 13. A car dealer advertises that he will pay 100% of the original cost of a car for a trade-in on a new van that costs $13,990. A purchaser trades in a car for which he paid $7,900. The car's actual current worth is $2,300. How much money did the buyer save on the trade in?

_____ 14. A major car manufacturer announced it paid $9,630,000,000 to 244,894 employees in one year. What was the average yearly wage for all employees?

_____ 15. The price of a Rolls-Royce Corniche II convertible is $168,000. The price of a Yugo is $3990. How many Yugos could you buy for one Corniche II? Approximately how many times more does the Corniche II cost than the Yugo?

_____ 16. Three car companies sold 217,939 automobiles in March, down 3.9% from a year ago. How many cars did they sell last year?

_____ 17. An automobile company planned to produce 85,000 cars, but due to buyer demand produced 125% of that number. How many cars did they produce?

_____ 18. In one city, the cost of owning and operating a compact car was $5,097. If the average miles driven for a year are 12,000, what was the cost per mile?

_____ 19. One company set aside $167,000,000 in bonuses for its top executives, but the payout was reduced by 30%. By how much was the payout reduced?

_____ 20. What was the amount of bonus money actually shared by the executives?

GA1610 Good Apple © 1997

Measurement Math

Take an Inch Page 5

1. 3,600
2. 3,937
3. 1,800
4. 1,128
5. 600
6. 4,680
7. 31,680,000

Take an Inch cont'd Page 6

8. 79,200
9. 726
10. 1,080
11. 1,577,790,720
12. 6,336,000
13. 136,857,600
14. 1,440,933,120
15. no

How Do You Measure Up? Page 7

1. b
2. c
3. c
4. b
5. b
6. c
7. a
8. c
9. b
10. a

How Do You Measure Up? cont'd Page 8

11. a
12. c
13. c
14. b
15. a
16. c
17. a
18. b
19. b
20. c

Measurement Match Page 9

1. d
2. h
3. f
4. j
5. b
6. c
7. i
8. g
9. a
10. e
11. m
12. n
13. r
14. p
15. q
16. s
17. t
18. k
19. l
20. o

Measurement Math Page 10

1. 160 acres
2. 102,400 sq. rods
3. 669,600,000 miles
4. 8 1/3 minutes
5. 1.29 seconds
6. $89.50
7. $2,471
8. 63,360 in.; 1,760 yd.
9. 4,620 feet
10. 1.77137 miles

Measurement Math cont'd Page 11

11. 100 acres
12. approx. 38 hours
13. 30 leagues (475,200 feet)
14. 34.7 days
15. $20
16. $126
17. $41.67
18. 11,000
19. Mary
20. 9 hours, 57 minutes, and 59 seconds

Metric Mathematics Page 12

1. 454 grams
2. 2.6 meters, 20.64 in.
3. 1,645.92 cm
4. 15,392.4 mm
5. 40.76 k
6. 1.788 in.
7. 96.6 km/hr
8. 104°F, 42°C, 113°F, 38°C
9. 3.8 liters in a gallon; 4.5 liters in an imperial gallon, $31.50

Matching Measurements Page 13

1. g
2. r
3. o
4. n
5. l
6. p
7. d
8. i
9. k
10. h
11. b
12. e
13. j
14. f
15. q
16. c
17. t
18. s
19. a
20. m

Money Math

Numismatic Numbers Page 14

1. $171.50, 88%
2. 86 times
3. $89,980
4. $1,750
5. $41.50
6. $83,200
7. $3.59
8. 4%
9. $11
10. no

Numismatic Numbers cont'd Page 15

11. $1
12. $1,820
13. 6¢
14. 31¢
15. $78
16. $1,360.80
17. $8.99
18. 91¢
19. $2.50
20. 5,181%

Family Budgets Page 16

1. $68,743
2. $71,133

3. $501.59
4. $632
5. $460.10
6. $961.69
7. 10.4%
8. 20.8%
9. 6.5%
10. $400

Family Budgets cont'd Page 17

11. a. $192.34
  b. $2,308.08
12. $278
13. $19.03
14. a. $57.70
  b. $3,000.47 based on take-home pay
15. $58,133
16. $11,857.24
17. $102,150
18. $98,500
19. $9,940, or approximately 10%
20. a. $41,200
  b. 10.7

Reading Stock Tables cont'd Page 19

1. $81.62 1/2
2. a. 1.20; b. .56
3. a. 186,300, b. 3,724,100, c. 232,700
4. a. lost $250, b. made $37.50, c. made $262.50, d. lost $25
5. a. Disney, b. Delta Air

Money Math Page 20

1. a. 18
  b. Washington
  c. Great Seal of United States
2. a. 2 years or 24 months
  b. Lincoln
  c. Lincoln Memorial
3. a. 36 years
  b. Jefferson
  c. Signing of Declaration of Independence.
4. a. 3 years or 36 months
  b. Alexander Hamilton
  c. United States Treasury
5. a. 60 months
  b. Andrew Jackson
  c. White House

Money Math cont'd Page 21

6. a. 9 years
  b. Ulysses S. Grant
  c. United States Capitol
7. a. 20 years
  b. Benjamin Franklin
  c. Independence Hall

8. a. 25%
   b. Bureau of Engraving and Printing
   c. Washington, D.C.
9. a. In God We Trust
   b. green
   c. 6" x 2 1/2"
10. a. 3/5
    b. Secret Service
    c. Treasurer of the United States and Secretary of the Treasury

Making Change — Page 22
1. $3.75: 3 quarters, 3 1-dollar bills
2. $5.85: 1 dime, 3 quarters, 1 5-dollar bill
3. $12.13: 3 pennies, 1 dime, 2 1-dollar bills, 1 10-dollar bill
4. $5.30: 1 nickel, 1 quarter, 1 5-dollar bill
5. $2.99: 4 pennies, 2 dimes, 3 quarters, 2 1-dollar bills
6. 58¢: 3 pennies, 1 nickel, 2 quarters
7. $2.97: 2 pennies, 2 dimes, 3 quarters, 2 1-dollar bills
8. 45¢: 2 dimes, 1 quarter
9. $3.15: 1 nickel, 1 dime, 3 1-dollar bills
10. $13.21: 1 penny, 2 dimes, 3 1-dollar bills, 1 10-dollar bill

Shopping Savvy — Page 23
cassette tape—99¢ savings; $15.01 change
shampoo—61¢ savings; $22.02 change
sweatshirt—$3.52 savings; $14.02 change
notebook—70¢ savings; $23.21 change
sunglasses—$1.61 savings; $18.11 change
decals—16¢ savings; $24.01 change
posters—51¢ savings; $21.02 change
mugs—51¢ savings; $21.53 change
backpacks—$2.40 savings; $5.01 change

Art's Appliances — Page 24
1. $409.98
2. $31.99
3. $17.01
4. $917.92
5. $59.98
6. $284.99

Tours by Train — Page 25
1. $99.50
2. $98.75
3. More – any reasonable answer
4. $1,990
5. $2,985

6. a. $790
   b. $1,185
7. $845.75
8. $335.75
9. $4,676.50
10. $1,856.50
11. 250 miles a day
12. 1,030 miles
13. 257.5 (257 1/2 miles)
14. Answers will vary.

Sports Math

Pictograph — Page 26
1. Monday, 150; Tuesday, 250; Wednesday, 125; Thursday, 350; Friday, 275; Saturday, 200
2. Thursday
3. Wednesday
4. Tuesday and Saturday
5. 225
6. 75
7. $300
8. $93.75
9. $262.50
10. $1,012.50

Baseball Math — Page 27
1. 360 feet
2. 8,100 sq. ft.
3. 900 sq. yd.
4. 720 ft.
5. 16 years
6. 3:52 p.m.
7. 90 players
8. 12 inches
9. 6,480 ft.
10. $53,185

Bicycle Numbers — Page 28
1. 79%
2. 2 days, 9 hours, 40 minutes
3. 3/5
4. non-exerciser 22.5 pounds, cyclist 12 pounds
5. 4 hours, 10 minutes
6. 8 hours, 20 minutes
7. 159,988 miles
8. 26.88 miles per year, 0.52 miles per week
9. $28,750,000
10. a) $137,400,000 b) $20,610,000
11. 65%
12. 22,000 miles
13. 13,807 miles

Basketball Math — Page 29
1. 90%
2. 520 free throws
3. 2,464 points
4. 32
5. 19%
6. 5.8 steals

7. 90% and 55%
8. Team B
9. 987 points
10. 340 rebounds

Basketball Math cont'd — Page 30
11. 1,107 field goals
12. 581.5 points
13. won 145, lost 82
14. $1,150,589.80
15. $16,012,800
16. 18.75%
17. 2-point shooter
18. 2.2 points
19. 395 inches
20. 30

Baseball Math — Page 31
1. .3050, .305
2. .3121, .312
3. .3258, .326
4. .2875, .288
5. .2753, .275

More Baseball Math — Page 32
1. 360 feet
2. 8,100 sq. ft.
3. 900 sq. yd.
4. 624 players
5. 13 games
6. 234 players
7. 158 years
8. 257,040 ft.
9. 48.68 miles (approx. 48 1/2 miles)

Spring Sports Facts — Page 33
1. 100; 2; 50
2. 80; 40; 160; 340
3. 19,704; $3.50; 9,852; $3

Sports Math — Page 34
1. 31 1/3 yards
2. 3 passes
3. 2160 inches
4. 30 feet per sec.
5. 75.6%
6. 388.9%
7. 26 points
8. Elaine
9. Linda
10. 37 1/2 m.p.h.

Sports Math cont'd — Page 35
11. under par
12. .333 batting average
13. 44.4%
14. 108 free throws
15. 10 bases
16. 4 hours
17. No, lost 15 to 12
18. 74
19. 4 hours
20. 16.7 hours

Football Pass — Page 36
1. A) W-13, B) W-31, C) W-25, D) W-46, E) S-45—Spartans' 45-yard line
2. A) S-17, B) S-15, C) S-41, D) W-43, E) 50—50-yard line
3. A) S-43, B) W-39, C) W-45, D) S-43, E) S-28—Spartans' 28-yard line

GA1610 Good Apple © 1997

4. A) W-42, B) W-35, C) W-37, D) W-28, E) W-0—Spartans made a touchdown at the Wildcats' 0-yard line

17. $30
18. 16,667 acres
19. 31 points
20. 390 points, 168 rebounds

16. F   17. Q   18. G
19. I   20. T   21. H
22. C   23. L   24. M
25. J

t's Baseball Time Again — Page 37

A. Tigers 75 2
   Lions 31 7
   Leopards 44 5
   Mice 69 3
   Rats 81 1
   Monkeys 38 6
   Moose 13 8
   Deer 50 4
B. Tom 30.8 7
   Mary 23.1 10
   Sam 31.1 6
   Dotti 27.5 8
   Mike 42.1 1
   Kim 25.9 9
   Tom 33.3 5
   Angie 34.6 4
   John 41.2 2
   Patti 37.5 3

Up to Bat — Page 38

Albert .325   Betsy .500
Carl .450   Diane .275
Ed .375   Felicia .400
Greg .350   Helen .300
Isaac .425

Par for the Course — Page 39

Hole #1 - 8   Hole #2 - 2
Hole #3 - 4   Hole #4 - 3
Hole #5 - 6   Hole #6 - 7
Hole #7 - 7   Hole #8 - 3
Hole #9 - 5
Total = 45   Par = 36

All Sports Math — Page 40

1. $16,333   2. $11,520
3. 192 baskets   4. 168 hits
5. 647 seconds   6. 100 runs
7. 5,061 feet   8. 2,475 lb.
9. 4.94 lb.   10. $43,666.67

All Sports Math cont'd — Page 41

11. .333 batting average
12. 24 inches
13. 5,000 acres
14. 14,667 tickets
15. 206 eagles
16. $2,000; $1,200; $800

Geometry

Finding Areas I — Page 43
1. 110.5 sq. ft.   2. 64 sq. ft.
3. 300 sq. yd.   4. 153.86 sq. ft.
5. 306.25 sq. in.   6. 25 sq. in.

Finding Areas II — Page 44
1. 763.02 sq. ft.   2. 500 sq. ft.
3. 144 sq. yd.   4. 174.5 sq. ft.
5. 32 sq. in.   6. 63 sq. ft.

Finding the Areas of Polygons Page 45
a. 3   b. 12   c. 4 1/2
d. 7 1/2   e. 4   f. 4
g. 12   h. 9   i. 2 1/2
j. 9   k. 8   l. 4
m. 17   n. 8   o. 5
p. 6   q. 8   r. 11
s. 11   t. 12

Triangular Spectacular — Page 46
C, D, F, M, and N

Line Designs — Page 47
2, 4, 5, 9, 13, 15

Geopuzzle — Page 49
1. triangle 180°
2. pentagon 540°
3. square 360°
4. rhombus 360°
5. hexagon 720°
6. circle 360°
7. parallelogram 360°
8. rectangle 360°
9. trapezoid 360°
10. octagon 1080°

Shaping Up — Page 50
B, F, H, M, O

Geometric Match-Up — Page 51
1. V   2. O   3. K
4. W   5. D   6. R
7. S   8. E   9. P
10. U   11. X   12. A
13. N   14. B   15. Y

Geometric Bubblegram — Page 52
1. angle   2. parallel
3. cone   4. segment
5. plane   6. intersection
7. circle   8. ray
9. line   10. square
11. face   12. cube
13. point   Geometry is fun!

The Shapes of Our Lives — Page 53
1. stop sign—octagon
2. pyramids—cones
3. billiard balls—spheres
4. pizzas—circles
5. football fields—rectangle
6. Pentagon—pentagon
7. sun—sphere
8. baseball diamond—diamond or square
9. rolling pin—cylinder
10. triangle—triangle
11. doughnuts—circles
12. bed—rectangle
13. pens, pencils—cylinders
14. doors—rectangles

Geometry Crossword Puzzle Page 54
Across
2. base   6. quadrangle
8. square   9. radius
12. rectangle   16. circumference
18. trapezoid   19. right angle
20. isosceles   21. rhombus
22. line   23. volume
24. plane   25. parallel
27. acute angle   28. geometry
31. reflex angle   33. height
34. polygons   35. intersecting
36. vertical   37. chord
Down
1. width   3. solid
4. parallelogram   5. cube
7. circle   10. arc
11. straight angle   13. scalene
14. diameter   15. triangle
17. curved   22. length
23. vertex   26. perimeter
29. obtuse   30. broken
32. cylinder

Scientific Math

Little Insects—Big Numbers   Page 55
1. 69 ants
2. 50,000 colonies
3. 775 weeks
4. 2,610,000 eggs
5. 12 1/2% species
6. 1.26%
7. 800 harmful
8. 60 times longer
9. 5 times slower
10. 250,000 females

Little Insects—Big Numbers cont'd   Page 56
11. 5,000,000 female houseflies
12. 7 1/2%
13. 10%
14. 1,200 flies; 400 mosquitoes
15. 625,000 species
16. 240 hours
17. 86,400 seconds
18. 54,749 days
19. 30 insect species
20. 10 small mosquitoes

Environmental Numbers   Page 57
1. 47 times
2. $491.80
3. 6%
4. 2,966 growth
5. 6 people
6. 15,800,000 deer
7. 7 key deer
8. 13.3%
9. 67.6%

Environmental Numbers cont'd   Page 58
10. 36,500 plants and animals
11. 15 stories tall
12. 30%
13. 107,500,000 acres
    3,071,429 acres lost
14. 4,000 landfills
15. 27.3 volunteers
16. 483.6 birds per species
17. 120 landfills

Solar System Numbers   Page 59
1. yes
2. a. 3,112,253 miles
   b. 92,956,131.5 years
3. a. 60 meteors; b. 420 meteors
4. 14.3%
5. a. 95; 10; b. 425 more
6. 3 times
7. 36,060,000 miles

Solar System Numbers cont'd   Page 60
8. 18,150 hours
9. 9 hours 16 minutes
10. a. 12.5 moons   b. 75 moons

11. a. 23,333 yards   b. 13 miles
12. 100,000,000
13. a. 10,500 miles   b. 630,000 miles
14. 20,000,000 revolutions
15. a. 4.2 times   b. 159.7 days
16. a. 840 feet   b. 112 feet

The Cost of Pollution   Page 61
1. 12,000,000 gallons
2. $18,750,000
3. $581,250,000; $562,500,000
4. 88 pounds
5. 17.6 pounds
6. 817,000 pounds
7. 6,347,000,000 pounds
8. 7,941,817,000 total pounds
9. 18.75%
10. 875,000,000 pounds

The Cost of Pollution cont'd   Page 62
11. 288,750,000 pounds
12. 26,000,000 trees
13. 60,000,000 plastic bottles
14. 1,860,000,000 plastic bottles
15. 96,000,000 acres
16. 1,000,000 (5 Sun. 1,250,000) trees
17. 17,534,247 barrels
18. 200,000 miles
19. 20,800 gallons
20. $26,000

Space Figures   Page 63
1. almost 26 years
2. 6 times more
3. $5,263,158
4. 1,600,000 miles
5. $75,000,000
6. $9,000,000,000
7. 80,000 spectators
8. 5,821 minutes
9. 3.67 people
10. $80,000

Space Figures cont'd   Page 64
11. 18,750 mph
12. 971,520 feet
13. 1,342.28 lb./ft.
.14. Oct. 5 at 1:20 p.m.
15. 24,574.79 lb./ft.
16. 1,352.46 lb./ft.
17. $20,408.16 per pound
18. 25,920 minutes
19. 1,184,000 of thrust
20. $178.57/mile

Go Figure!   Page 65
1. 8 hours working x 24 quarts per minute x 60 minutes = 11,520 quarts.
   16 hours resting x 3 quarts per minute x 60 minutes = 2,880 quarts or 14,400 quarts per day.
   14,400 quarts per day x 7 days per week = 100,800 quarts per week.
   14,400 quarts per day x 30 days per month = 432,000 quarts per month.
   14,440 quarts per day x 365 days per year = 5,256,000 quarts per year.
2. 2,000 pounds per ton x 10 tons per day = 20,000 pounds per day.
   20,000 pounds per day x 7 days per week = 140,000 pounds per week.
   20,000 pound per day x 30 days per month = 600,000 pounds per month.
   20,000 pounds per day x 365 days per year = 7,300,000 pounds per year.
3. Earth's diameter = 7,927 miles.
   Earth's circumference = pi (3.14) x diameter = 24,890.78
   60,000 ÷ 24,891 = more than two times. (2.4)
   Moon's diameter = 2,160 miles.
   Moon's circumference = pi x diameter = 6,782.4
   60,000 ÷ 6,782 = almost 9 times.
4. 66.6 feet; 22.22 yards

Dinosaur Math   Page 66
1. 160,000 pounds
2. 2.22 times taller
3. the thoroughbred horse
4. dinosaurs 5 minutes, humans 4 miles
5. 49.20 feet
6. approximately 8 humans (7.9)
7. 26.66 times longer
8. 145 million years

Dinosaur Math cont'd   Page 67
9. 9,855 more days
10. approximately 4 (4.2)
11. 16 human teeth
12. 62 1/2 sets
13. 2 1/2%
14. 10 feet

GA1610 Good Apple © 1997

15. 3 times
16. 140,000 pounds

Graph It!   **Page 68**
Answers will vary.

Cleaning Up Our Home   Page 69
Spaceship Earth is the only home we have. It's counting on us to do everything we can to protect it.

Historical Math

Math History   Page 70
1. 1788 (1775 + 13)
2. 3563 (1776 + 1787)
3. 450 (200 + 150 + 100)
4. 544 (435 + 100 + 9)
5. 3227 (1607 + 1620)
6. 37 (50 – 13)
7. 85 (1861 – 1776)
8. 37 (42 – 5)
9. 0 (nineteenth century 4, twentieth century 4)
10. 2 (42 – 40 signers of Constitution)

Math History cont'd   Page 71
11. 176 (22 x 8)
12. 100 (50 x 2)
13. 2 (2;2;2)
14. 2/3
15. 5.3 years
16. 19%
17. 2.4%; 100% (only one Confederate president)
18. 15 (7 Ohio, 8 Virginia)
19. Adams - 1735, Jefferson - 1743

Edison Math   Page 72
1. $1739.13
2. 16.66 or 16 years, 7 months, 2 days
3. $66,640
4. .0023 cents
5. a. $32,000 weekly,
   b. $1,600,000 yearly
6. 660
7. 105.6 days
8. $95,238.10
9. $202,380.95
10. $107,142.85
11. 33.3%
12. 58 years
13. 43 years old
14. 69.05%
15. a. 50 years, b. 82 years old

Martin Luther King, Jr.'s Life in Numbers   Page 73
1. 53%   2. 141
3. 6,494,000 fares   4. $1,298,800
5. 1,222 to 1   6. 10,000,000 mi.
7. 42 times   8. 1,350,000 mi.
9. 20%   10. $1,542.86

Important Dates in Marie Curie's Life   Page 74
N - 1904   E - 1903
I - 1883   H - 1895
L - 1898   T - 1891
P - 1867   B - 1897
D - 1911   C - 1893
              E - 1934

Mystery Word: Pitchblende
Significance: When Marie was studying radiation, she discovered that the ore, pitchblende, gave off more radiation than could be accounted for by known elements. She was therefore led to believe that the ore contained a new element. The existence of another element was contrary to current beliefs in the area of physics. Marie's work with pitchblende led her on the path to discovering two new elements, which she named polonium and radium.

The Wright Brothers   Page 75
1. 4 years old
2. 1878
3. Wilbur-33 yrs. old, Orville-29 yrs. old
4. Wilbur-28 yrs. old, Orville-24 yrs. old
5. 36 years old
6. 37 years old
7. 41 years old
8. In 1873 Wilbur was 6; Orville was 2.
9. In 1875 Wilbur was 8; Orville was 4.
10. Wilbur—45 yrs. old, Orville—77 yrs. old

Grandma Moses' Math   Page 76
1. $58
2. $26
3. 50¢
4. 20¢
5. a. feed, straw, shelter, milking equipment, fence, etc.

b. feed, straw, shelter, pen, etc.
6. a. 3 boxes   b. 5 boxes
7. a. 420 bottles   b. 21 boxes
8. a. 700 bottles   b. 35 boxes
9. 80 prints or pounds
10. 160 prints or pounds

Grandma Moses' Math cont'd Page 77
11. a. $24
    b. $32   c. $80
12. a. $1.25   b. $2.50
13. a. $1.50   b. $3.00
14. 5 barrels
15. 8 gallons
16. Young people got together to stir mixture; perhaps women worked together, also.
17. 90 trips
18. seed or plants, fertilizer, labor, etc.
19. potatoes, sweet potatoes, beans, squash, corn, pumpkin, okra

Presidential Mathematics   Page 78
1. Pierce
2. 221
3. 123 (remember Cleveland's non-consecutive terms)
4. 10/42, or 5/21
5. about 80
6. 31%
7. 8.4%
8. 74 years, 9 months, and 10 days

Inauguration Ages   Page 79
1. 57   2. 61   3. 57
4. 57   5. 58   6. 57
7. 61   8. 54   9. 68
10. 51   11. 49   12. 64
13. 50   14. 48   15. 65
16. 52   17. 56   18. 46
19. 54   20. 49   21. 51
22. 47   23. 55   24. 54
25. 42   26. 51   27. 56
28. 55   29. 51   30. 54
31. 51   32. 60   33. 62
34. 43   35. 55   36. 56
37. 61   38. 52   39. 69
40. 64   41. 46
1. Theodore Roosevelt
2. 1
3. Ronald Reagan
4. John F. Kennedy; Ronald Reagan
5. 17 years

McGuffey's Math **Page 80**
1. 1,452,381 Readers 2. $91,500,000
3. $9,150,000 4. 876 months
5. 44 years 6. $78
7. 20% 8. 46.1%
9. 33 1/3%

McGuffey's Math cont'd **Page 81**
10. 5 times 11. 33 dog stories
12. 47.95% 13. 84.21%
14. 7.69% 15. 33 1/3%
16. 194 candles 17. 73 years old
18. a. 28 years old b. 44 years old

Civil War Numbers **Page 82**
1. 59.4%
2. 56 years, 63 days
3. 90.9%
4. 403,151 more votes
5. 72.2%
6. 17 years, 124 days
7. 3 years, 362 days
8. 36%
9. 5.9%
10. 20%

Civil War Numbers cont'd **Page 83**
11. 620,000
12. 165,000
13. 20%
14. 26.7%
15. 6%
16. 13%
17. same
18. 182 years, 60.7 years
19. 63%
20. 7.42 times

Trail Math **Page 84**
1. 18 cents
2. 529,911,680
3. 3 cents
4. 250 days
5. a. 48 mph b. 500 mph
6. 4.3 oxen per wagon
7. 2.6 people per wagon
8. a. $197,000,000 b. $65,666,666
9. 17.8 miles
10. $1,270,000,000

Trail Math cont'd **Page 85**
11. 8.8 times
12. 1.19 elk
13. 37.5 wagons

14. a. 645 times b. 496 times
15. a. 122 people b. 27 wagons
16. 56 cents
17. $8,500
18. $46,250
19. $34,000
20. $5,625,000

A Romp With Roman Numerals **Page 86**
1. 8 x 5 = 40 (XL)
2. 33 + 17 = 50 (L)
3. 69 − 11 = 58 (LVIII)
4. 100 + 110 + 140 = 350 (CCCL)
5. 3000 − 1700 = 1300 (MCCC)
6. 999 ÷ 3 = 333 (CCCXXXIII)
7. 718 − 187 = 531 (DXXXI)
8. 575 + 2644 = 3219 (MMMCCXIX)

1. $\overline{\text{X}}$ 2. $\overline{\text{XXV}}$
3. $\overline{\text{L}}$ 4. $\overline{\text{C}}$
5. $\overline{\text{M}}$ 6. $\overline{\text{MV}}$
7. $\overline{\text{MX}}$ 8. $\overline{\text{X}}$MMMDXXIV

10,884

Mythology Design: Apollo, God of the Sun **Page 87**

Mayan Numbers **Page 88**
5 + 8 = 13 11 + 6 = 17
16 − 9 = 7 12 − 4 = 8
3 x 5 = 15 0 x 17 = 0
16 ÷ 4 = 4 10 ÷ 2 = 5
19 + 0 = 19 9 x 2 = 18
15 − 13 = 2 18 ÷ 9 = 2

Car Computing **Page 89**
1. $6,695
2. $247.72
3. 241 wks., 60 1/4 mos.
4. $1,634.75
5. Car A
6. $31.56
7. $6,834.52
8. the car with rebate
9. car with transportation charges included
10. 15.5%

Car Computing cont'd **Page 90**
11. 17%
12. $16,395
13. $5,600
14. $39,323.14
15. 42 Yugos, 42 times more
16. 226,784 cars
17. 106,250 cars
18. 42 cents
19. $50,100,000
20. $116,900,000

GA1610 Good Apple © 1997